THE CUP OF
SALVATION

A Manual for Eucharistic Ministers

BETH WICKENBERG ELY

Morehouse Publishing
NEW YORK · HARRISBURG · DENVER

A FORMATION TRINITY

In loving memory of Daddy: A TDB of my own!

To CREDO: Behold my BHAG!

In grateful thanksgiving for Jim Fenhagen+:
Rector, dean, mentor, friend

"Well done, good and faithful servant"

Morehouse Publishing, 4775 Linglestown Road, Harrisburg, PA 17112

Morehouse Publishing, 445 Fifth Avenue, New York, NY 10016

Morehouse Publishing is an imprint of Church Publishing Incorporated.
www.churchpublishing.org

Cover design by Laurie Klein Westhafer

Typeset by Rose Design

Library of Congress Cataloging-in-Publication Data

Ely, Elizabeth Wickenberg.
 The cup of salvation : a manual for Eucharistic ministers / Beth Wickenberg Ely.
    p. cm.
 Includes bibliographical references (p.   ).
 ISBN 978-0-8192-2814-7 (pbk.) -- ISBN 978-0-8192-2815-4 (ebook) 1.
Lord's Supper--Lay administration--Episcopal Church. I. Title.
 BX5949.C5E48 2012
 264'.03036--dc23
                                    2012023781

Printed in the United States of America

CONTENTS

FOREWORD

There is a real sense in which the community of Jesus gathers to worship God and then scatters to witness to the God we worship, in the world. Genuine worship is not a way of escape but way of deeper engagement in the world. That is one of the messages of the book of Hebrews in the New Testament and why *Cup of Salvation* is such an incredible gift to the Church in our time and age.

One might argue that Hebrews is an extended meditation on the power of the worship of God to impact our lives for the good, and through us, to impact the world for the good. The entire eleventh chapter of Hebrews, in the poetic meter of a preacher, calls the roll of biblical people whose lives of lived faithfulness to God and God's way of love changed the world for the better, pushing it closer to God's dream for us and all creation. But before telling of these people, the writer declares that the faithful and authentic worship of God is the way that leads to faithful lives that witness and make a difference in the world. The writer says it this way:

> And let us consider how to provoke one another to love and good deeds, not neglecting to meet together, as is the habit of some, but encouraging one another, and all the more as you see the Day approaching. (Hebrews 10:24–25)

Commenting on this passage pastor and theologian Brian McLaren writes:

We meet together to encourage one another and "to provoke one another to love and good deeds" (Hebrews 10:24). In other words, when the community of faith gathers, its purpose is to equip its members for a life of love and good deeds when the community scatters.[1]

Canon Beth Ely tells the story of our faith, the story of our way of worship, the story of baptized disciples in our Episcopal tradition serving one another in order that we might serve the world in Jesus' Name. She tells the story in the spirit of that old Gospel song of Fannie Crosby. "This is my story, this is my song, praising my Savior all the day long." The book, frankly, sings more as it reads. It teaches. It preaches. It prays to the One we worship and in whose Name we dare to witness and strive to serve. This is, in the spirit of Hebrews 10:24, a provocative book. It is a book that I pray will provoke us to a way of worship that leads us to witness in the world in the Name of Jesus.

"And let us consider how to provoke one another to love and good deeds, not neglecting to meet together, as is the habit of some, but encouraging one another. . . ."

—Michael B. Curry
Bishop of North Carolina

---

1. Brian McLaren, *Finding Our Way Again: The Return of the Ancient Practices* (Nashville: Thomas Nelson, 2008), 113.

INTRODUCTION

You are God's viceroy, God's representative.
You are God's stand-in, a God Carrier.
You are precious; God depends on you.
God believes in you and has no one but you
To do the things that only you can do for God.
Become what you are.

—**Archbishop Desmond Tutu**[1]

The lay office of Eucharistic Minister is fairly new to the church, having been inscribed into canon in 1985 by General Convention. It is stunning, really, that this ministry has evolved so much even since that time. We who serve the One to whom a "day is like a thousand years, and a thousand years are like a day" (2 Peter 3:8) have grown used to the excruciatingly slow pace of change in our much beloved Episcopal Church. Yet the rapidly developing identity of Eucharistic Ministers—the who, what, when, and how they are to serve—reflects a mighty shift in the theology of the laity. Things are still in flux, the last a 2003 change in the title of the ministry, from Lay Eucharistic Minister to Eucharistic Minister.

I remember as a child that the only laypeople I saw near the altar were acolytes. At that time, all acolytes

---

1. "Discernment Brochure 2010," Episcopal Diocese of Oregon, accessed January 22, 2012, *http://www.episcopaldioceseoregon.org/files/discernment_brochure_2010.pdf.*

were boys and men. Like many other little girls before me, I longed to be at the altar. At that time, the longing expressed itself as a desire to serve God as acolyte—to carry that heavy cross down the aisle leading the procession, to help the priest set the table by handing him the silver and glass containers in the proper order and assisting as he washed his hands.

I well remember when laywomen first were allowed to read God's Word from behind the big eagle holding the Bible. All of a sudden, it seemed, girls were acolytes, too, but by then I was too old. Then adult laypeople were vested and sitting in the chancel with the clergy as a part of the service. People who were not bishops, priests, or deacons—both men and women—began serving the chalice at the altar rail! That, I thought, would be the most sublime ministry of all, actually being able to offer the Cup of Salvation to God's people and to help them drink of it.

Today, every Sunday across The Episcopal Church and throughout the world where Anglicanism reaches, Eucharistic Ministers take up the chalice to help commune the people of God. They take part in the service from the chancel as laypeople, representing the majority of God's people (there are far more laypeople than clergy!) and the dignity of their order of ministry.

Including the laity as ministers of the sacrament sends a startling message the church has not heard since Christianity was young: that laypeople are rightful bearers of the gifts in the eucharist; that the sacrament of holy communion is not too sacred for lay hands; that laity are responsible and cognizant enough of the gravity of the task to take up their legitimate ministry of its distribution.

Since I wrote my first book on lay sacramental ministry in the late 1980s, *A Manual for Lay Eucharistic Ministers* (now called *A Manual for Eucharistic Visitors*), I have been waiting for someone else to write another about the lay ministry that once was considered its partner: those who help distribute the sacrament (most commonly the cup) at services. Often colloquially called chalice bearers or chalicists, these are now designated by canon as Eucharistic Ministers. Thus I will be using the abbreviated forms EM and EMs.

Evidently I was the one called to write this second book, and so I have, trying to include theological, practical, and just-plain-interesting information about the eucharist for those laypeople called to minister sacramentally.

One of the best things about this ministry is that women never have been restricted from carrying it out, and I have tried to use inclusive language in this book. I have attempted to be thoroughly Anglican in my theology, so if there is heresy here, I will quickly recant. Good people of faith will disagree about many topics and interpretations within these pages. That is a sign of these turbulent times in which I believe "God is working his purpose out." The practical advice and observations are from my own and others' experiences with this ministry since its inception. You, your clergy, and your bishop may reject and shudder at some of my suggestions. Obey your clergy and bishop, please, for they are the ones who have charge over you.

The many dimensions of this subject have proved fascinating. It is long past the time that the church recognizes the immense impact this ministry has had, not only on the institution itself but on the many faithful laypeople who have answered the call and continue to help us give liturgical witness to our Anglican theology of the equality of all orders of ministry.

Many thanks, as always to my husband, Duncan Cairnes Ely; our son, Penn Wickenberg Ely; and our ever-faithful canine family, Gravatt, Moses, and Saxon, who don't care how the book is going. Deepest gratitude also goes to my editor, Nancy Bryan, who had to move from Chapel Hill to New York so that we could "meet," and who is unusually accepting of my prose and "creative" ideas.

—The Rev. Canon Beth Wickenberg Ely+
"Dunwyck"
Columbus, NC
First Sunday in Lent
February 26, 2012

EUCHARIST

t is truly extraordinary that in The Episcopal Church the laity now can receive the body of Christ in their hands and the blood from the chalice, both administered by another layperson. The confluence of these developments—communion in two kinds; the body received in the hands; and laypeople distributing the sacrament as licensed Eucharistic Ministers—is theologically revolutionary.

The earliest Christians handled the body and blood freely. Lay Christians routinely took the bread home with them from the Sunday eucharist, where they kept it nearby in case of emergency. Life in ancient times was tenuous. An accident that would seem trivial today could kill a person. Childbirth was just as likely to cause death to the mother as the infant, or both. Any journey was fraught with dangers of accidents, bandits, getting lost, and falling ill. A cooking mishap could be fatal. The faithful wanted to make sure they had access to communion in an emergency when a priest could not be found, thus you have laypeople communicating themselves and others with the consecrated ele-

1

ments. Deacons and laypeople also took communion to the sick during the week.[1]

The early Christians also treated the sacrament like a lucky charm, and some carried it around their neck in a pouch to ward off danger and evil. An early story tells of Satyrus, who was on a sea voyage. When his ship wrecked, he tied the sacrament around his neck, jumped into the sea, and credited its presence for saving him from a certain death.[2]

The earliest Christians probably received bread in their right hand, kissing it and moving it to their own mouths. From about the fourth century, women were required to wrap a cloth around their right hand in order to receive. Some laity drank the wine directly from the chalice and others through a small tube or *fistula*. These early practices were not uniform.

One of the earliest writers, St. Cyril of Jerusalem (ca. 313–86), gives a blueprint for faithful reception of the body and the blood:

> In approaching therefore, come not with thy wrists extended, or thy fingers spread; but make thy left hand a throne for the right, as for that which is to receive a King. And having hollowed thy palm, receive the Body of Christ, saying over it, *Amen*. So then after having carefully hallowed thine eyes by the touch of the Holy Body, partake of it; giving heed lest thou lose any portion thereof. . . .

---

1. Mike Aquilina, *The Mass of the Early Christians* (Huntington, IN: Our Sunday Visitor, 2001), 41.

2. Beth Wickenberg Ely, *A Manual for Eucharistic Visitors* (Harrisburg, PA: Morehouse, 2005), 2.

Then after thou hast partaken of the Body of Christ,
draw near also to the Cup of His Blood; not stretching
forth thine hands, but bending, and saying with an air of
worship and reverence, *Amen*, hallow thyself by partak-
ing also of the Blood of Christ. And while the moisture is
still upon thy lips, touch it with thine hands, and hallow
thine eyes and brow and the other organs of sense.[3]

But writing at the same time as St. Cyril, St. Basil of
Caesarea (330–79) tells us that receiving the bread in the
hand is only allowed in times of persecution.[4] He suggests
what many other writers do: that reception of the eucharist
on the tongue is the norm.

■ ACCESS LIMITED

As the church became what we know as the Church, the
increasing number of converts necessitated further organiza-
tion. The Church began to set aside (ordained) leaders, and
the clergy began to restrict the laity's access to the eucharist,
probably for reasons of safeguarding something sacred and
regulating its proper use.

Thus, the clergy became the guardians of the sacraments, and probably by the late fourth century, the laity
did not routinely remove the bread and the wine from the
service. What's more, by church decree three hundred years

3. Cyril of Jerusalem, "Mystagogical Catechesis" V:21-22, in *Nicene and Post-Nicene Fathers of the Christian Church*, Series II, vol. VII, eds. Philip Schaff and Henry Wace, trans. Edwin Hamilton Gifford (Edinburgh: T&T Clark, 1893) 400-401. *http://www.ccel.org/ccel/schaff/npnf207.pdf.*
4. Basil the Great, "Letter 93," in *Nicene and Post-Nicene Fathers of the Christian Church*, Series II, vol. III, eds. Philip Schaff and Henry Wace, trans. Blomfield Jackson (Edinburgh: T&T Clark, 1894) 526. *http://www.ccel.org/ccel/schaff/npnf208.pdf.*

later, the laity no longer were allowed to even touch the elements. One of the theological reasons given was that only something that was consecrated (the priest's hands anointed at ordination) should touch the body and blood, and thus the paten and the cup. No one but a priest or a bishop (not even a deacon) was ordinarily even allowed to remove from or to place anything upon the holy altar.

St. Thomas Aquinas makes the reasons for this very clear much later, in the mid-thirteenth century:

> Out of reverence towards this sacrament, nothing touches it but what is consecrated, hence the corporal and the chalice are consecrated, and likewise the priest's hands, for touching this sacrament. Hence it is not lawful for anyone to touch it, except from necessity, for instance if it were to fall upon the ground, or else in some other case of urgency.[5]

This idea that the consecrated hands of the priests and bishops were the only ones holy enough to touch the eucharist became the basis for placing the body on the communicant's tongue instead of in her palm, although it was not a universal practice until a church decree in 650.

Finally, a council at Rouen in 650 settled the matter, decreeing, "Do not put the Eucharist in the hands of any layman or laywomen but only in their mouths."[6] A mere forty-two years later, a council in Constantinople prohibited laity from giving themselves communion, thus stopping completely the practice of taking it home and/or receiving it even when

---

5. Thomas Aquinas, *Summa Theologica*, Vol. III, 82,13, trans. Fathers of the English Dominican Province (New York: Benziger Brothers, 1947).

6. "Communion in the Hand Is a Sacrilege," These Last Days Ministries, accessed February 24, 2012, *http://www.tldm.org/news2/cih.htm.*

the clergy put it into their own hands.[7] Meanwhile, the clergy always ate the body and drank the precious blood.

Though in most of the rest of the world, Roman Catholics still receive the bread upon their tongues, in 1977 Pope Paul VI allowed the U.S. Bishops to return to the practice of giving the host into communicants' palms.

■ DOCTRINE OF CONCOMITANCE

Anglicans have been receiving both the bread and wine since the founding of the Church of England in the sixteenth century. For the Reformers, one of the problems with Roman Catholicism was that the elements were not available in both "kinds" or "species."

The Council of Trent (1545) put forth the Doctrine of Concomitance in reaction to the Reformers' insistence that the laity have access to the cup. Anglicans, like Roman Catholics, still uphold this doctrine, which says that the consecrated bread and wine each contain entirely both the body and blood of Christ. A congregant who just receives the bread or just receives the wine has received Christ in the body and the blood.

SPIRITUAL COMMUNION

Spiritual Communion is a communion of desire, meaning that a Christian inwardly shares in the eucharist, though the body and blood are not physically present.

---

7. Henri LeClercq and Fernand Cabrol, "Communion," in *Dictionnaire d'Archéologie Chrétienne et de Liturgie*, vol. 3, part 2 (Paris: Librarie Letouzey et Ané, 1948), 2570.

> In 2001, the bishops of the Church of England reiterated that the Anglican Church subscribes to the "ancient Catholic teaching that a person prevented from receiving the sacred elements may be brought into real communion with our Lord through faith ('Believe and you have eaten,' as St. Augustine says), just as the whole Christ is received when communion is administered in one kind."[8]
>
> The first BCP (1549) recommended spiritual communion for those who could not attend because of illness or for those who could not swallow the elements. Eucharistic Visitors now take care of many of these pastoral situations.

Why does this matter to Eucharistic Ministers?

Often EMs serve persons at the altar rail who choose to receive only the bread or (less often) only the wine. Thus, EMs who are aware of this doctrine can assure alcoholics who abstain from the consecrated wine, for instance, that they have received the fullness of communion in the bread. Conversely, people who drink only the consecrated wine because they cannot digest the gluten in the bread used for the eucharist, have also received the full benefit of communion.

The English Reformers held out for the necessity of the bread and the cup to be available to all. From the beginning of the English Church, Article XXX of the Articles of Religion (1571) stated: "The Cup of the Lord is not to be denied to the Lay-people: for both the parts of the Lord's Sacrament, by Christ's ordinance and commandment, ought to be ministered to all Christian men alike."[9]

---

8. House of Bishops of the Church of England 2001.

9. The Episcopal Church, *The Book of Common Prayer and Administration of the Sacraments and Other Rites and Ceremonies of the Church* (New York: Church Hymnal Corp., 1979), 874. Hereafter referred to as BCP.

■ "CHURCHPERSONSHIP," FORMERLY KNOWN AS "CHURCHMANSHIP"

In the mid-twentieth century, Sunday schools and camps often taught various versions of this song to illustrate some of the truths of our Anglican identity:

I Am an Anglican
Sung to "God Bless America"
Author: probably wanted to remain anonymous

I am an Anglican.
I am P.E. *(Protestant Episcopal)*
I am High Church,
And Low Church
I am Protestant and Catholic and free.
Not a Presby,
Nor a Luth'ran
Nor a Baptist, white with foam.
I am an Anglican,
Just one step from Rome.
I am an Anglican,
Via media's my home.

Using this lighthearted synopsis, here is a very brief sketch of some of the areas in which we differ but remain wonderfully—and even miraculously—united.

People who visit Episcopal churches often wonder how services using the same *Book of Common Prayer* can contain so much variety. Shouldn't it always be exactly the same? Thankfully, not so! Styles of worship often differ, and these differences reflect some very real theological differences within our one denomination. The old-school way of referring to these differences was High Church, Low Church (see song above), and Broad Church—or churchmanship.

This word still has not really changed. Although Episcopalians are more aware of inclusive language than ever, "churchpersonship" is a mouthful!

One way of looking at Episcopalians is along a spectrum with Protestant on one end and Roman Catholic on the other. Such a spectrum has nothing to do with a conservative/liberal range but is a spiritual orientation. As a matter of fact, the Anglican Church is the only church to claim to be both Protestant and Catholic at the same time, since it is a product of an (English) Reformation (a "Protestant" is one who protests) as surely as are our Lutheran brothers and sisters. On the other hand, we use the term "Catholic" in much the same way as the "Roman Catholic" church originally used it starting in the fifteenth century—to mean "universal."

Along that spectrum from High Church to Low Church is a middle ground often referred to as Broad Church. Episcopalians are famous for taking the *via media,* or middle way, the gift of being able to seek a balance of views instead of seeing black and white or right and wrong. So a great many of our congregations are what we call Broad Church.

Congregations that are High Church are closer to the Roman Catholic or Eastern Orthodox end of the spectrum. They use icons and "smells and bells" (incense and sanctus bells) in chanted liturgies. Their vestments and other trappings can be breathtaking, and some lucky laypersons (subdeacons) get to wear and use them! Some of these Episcopal churches even add historical elements to services, such as the *Angelus.* This High Church orientation is also known as Anglo-Catholic.

Broad Church is in the middle and combines elements of High and Low churches. These congregations might use incense on festive occasions such as Christmas and Easter and maybe some feast days; yet priestly vestments usually are minimal and hymns tend to be a mixture of "old" and "new" and sometimes from supplemental Episcopal hymnals.

Low Church congregations come out of a distinctly Protestant Evangelical orientation. In fact, except for the cadences of *The Book of Common Prayer*, a worshipper might think he is in a United Methodist Church. (After all, members of the Wesley family were devoted members of the Church of England!) These parishes often are plain inside, they do not usually reserve the sacrament, and their liturgies are less formal. They might be more inclined to have what we call today "contemporary services." The music might include many hymns from the renewal movement.

But all these churches—High, Broad, and Low—are Episcopalian! Pick the style that speaks to your heart. This is one of the great things about being a part of The Episcopal Church! By no means are we cookie-cutter congregations.

■ THE DOCTRINE OF THE REAL PRESENCE

Episcopalians believe that the bread and wine become the body and blood of Christ. Theologians have debated for centuries just how that happens and what it means.

The Episcopal Church's official position on this is called the Doctrine of the Real Presence. The following definition is by Thomas Aquinas: "The whole Christ is present under every part or quantity of each species. As a loaf of bread is *bread,* and a slice of bread is *bread,* and a crumb of bread is *bread,* so, the Eucharistic species, in whatever quantity, is Christ."[10]

Each crumb of bread contains the whole of Christ, like each piece of a fractal pattern contains the whole of the pattern, no matter how small.

St. Cyril cautions:

> . . . for whatever thou losest, is evidently a loss to thee as it were from one of thine own members. For tell me, if any one gave thee grains of gold, wouldest thou not hold them with all carefulness, being on thy guard against losing any of them, and suffering loss? Wilt thou not then much more carefully keep watch, that not a crumb fall from thee of what is more precious than gold and precious stones?[11]

Thus, we treat the consecrated bread and wine as we would Christ himself: with reverence for his holiness. This means many Episcopal clergy and laity believe that crumbs from the bread are considered to be the body, and like the entire wafer, not to be scattered or stepped on but quickly retrieved if they are dropped. Anglo-Catholic clergy are particularly aware of this. One of the reasons it is difficult to serve loaf bread is that it has a lot more crumbs than wafers. The same care is taken with wine that spills.

WHY I LIKE COMMUNION WAFERS . . .

1. Do not have to be chewed
2. Few if any crumbs
3. Easier to count when setting up for eucharist

10. Aquinas, *Summa Theologica,* III, 76, 3a.
11. Cyril, "Mystagogical Catechesis," V:21, 400.

4. Easier to estimate how many if I don't count them

5. Never distribute too big a piece for someone to swallow

6. Easier to consume if I over count

7. Can usually consume extras without wine

8. Don't usually have to break them as I distribute them

9. If we have the right kind, those with celiac disease can receive them

10. Fit better on a paten

11. Easier to pick up from the paten

12. More sanitary

13. Easier to pick up off the floor if dropped

14. Easier to fish out of a chalice if dropped in it

15. Communion doesn't take as long

16. Don't spoil when reserved in aumbry or tabernacle

Oh yes, Episcopalians differ in their theology, usually as a part of their "churchpersonship." Our ability to include people of such widely divergent views has long been the strength of Anglicanism.

WHY I DON'T LIKE COMMUNION WAFERS . . .

1. Don't taste as good as loaf bread

2. Probably weren't used at the Last Supper

3. Probably not made by someone I know who has prayed over it as she kneaded and baked it and gave it as a gift for our eucharist

4. Slide off of a flat paten

5. Blow off a flat paten when I walk with it

6. Hard to pick up off the paten with long fingernails
7. All the monks' good recipes are for altar bread
8. Don't remotely look like real bread, which puzzles children when we say "The Bread of Christ"

Anglicans' Doctrine of the Real Presence acknowledges a change in the elements of communion though not a belief that Christ is present materially. Thus the doctrine is broad enough to encompass a variety of other ways of looking at what happens when the bread and wine are consecrated.

Episcopal churches worship according to their eucharistic theologies. For example, the theology of Anglo-Catholic churches is closest to that of the Roman Catholic Church, which holds to the doctrine of *transubstantiation,* a form of the Doctrine of the Real Presence. *Transubstantiation* maintains that God converts the bread and wine into the body and blood during the Prayer of Consecration, though their material substance is not changed.

Low churches often have a more Protestant understanding and reject any notion that the body and blood changes into the bread and the wine. Instead they focus on the spiritual presence of Christ in the elements that can only be received by the faithful, agreeing with the ideas developed by Jeremy Taylor, a seventeenth-century Anglican bishop that it may not be about a change of substance, but it is about a substantial change.[12]

Incarnational theology is especially important to Broad Church Episcopalians, who treasure the truth that the eternal

---

12. Jeremy Taylor, "Of the Real Presence of Christ in the Holy Sacrament," in *The Whole Works of the Right Reverend Jeremy Taylor,* vol. VI, sec. I, ed. Reginald Heber, rev. Charles Page Eden (London: Longman, Brown, Green, and Longmans, 1852), 14.

Christ makes himself known through very earthly elements—bread and wine. They often embrace the question of how Christ is present in the eucharist as a deep mystery.

> **"He was the Word that spake it;**
> **He took the bread and brake it;**
> **And what that Word did make it;**
> **I do believe and take it."**[13]

▪ NAMING OUR WORSHIP

The names we give to our worship services reflect our theologies, just as the ways we conduct our worship services do:

- eucharist or holy eucharist
- communion or holy communion
- the Lord's supper
- the mass
- the liturgy or the divine liturgy

Each of these terms is correct, and each stresses a different prism through which believers look upon the divine mystery of what happens when they partake of the body and blood.

Low Churches often call their service the "Lord's supper," which emphasizes the historical remembrance of the service, which some see as a memorial or anniversary celebration of what once happened.

13. John Donne, "On the Sacrament," in *Remembering the Faith: What Christians Believe*, by Douglas J. Brouwer (Grand Rapids, MI: Wm. B. Eerdmans, 1999), 131.

"Communion" and "holy communion" reflect the unitive nature of the sacrament, in that the recipient joins with Christ when she partakes of the bread and wine, and that the community becomes one with each other and with the larger Body of Christ. In this way, Christ is made present once again, not as a memory, but in a mystical way that allows the believer to enter into his birth, death, and resurrection. This is referred to as "anamnesis."

The terms "holy eucharist" and "eucharist" ("thanksgiving" in Greek) emphasize the gratitude of the faithful for everything God has given and is giving, particularly Christ's sacrifice on the cross for the salvation of the world.

High Churches use the word "mass," which is what Roman Catholics call their sacramental liturgy. This word comes from the end of the service in which the faithful are sent out to do the work of God. The Latin phrase is "*Ite, missa est*," "Go, the mass is ended."

Orthodox Christians also use "the liturgy" and the "divine liturgy." These terms place an emphasis on the worship itself as a gateway to heaven and access to God through Jesus Christ.

Each of these labels carries with it a truth but none contains the whole of the truth of this sacrament, which has layers upon layers of meaning. In fact, the holy eucharist is so mystical we will never get to the bottom of its affects and its effects on this side of the kingdom. Nor are we meant to.

I often picture the eucharist as like the divine puff pastry known as Napoleons or *mille-feuilles*. Those "thousand sheets" are impossible to count because they are not meant to be dissected. They are meant to be savored. I am sure *mille-feuilles* is served at the heavenly banquet!

■ GUESS WHO'S COMING TO SUPPER?

The Lord's supper, that is. Though we often don't think of it this way, we who are the baptized are the guests at the Lord's supper. We are the blessed ones invited to the "marriage supper of the Lamb" (Revelation 19:9). The presider issues God's invitation each week: "The gifts of God for the People of God" (BCP, p. 365), holding out the bread and wine in invitation.

In our theological understanding, Christ always is the host of our eucharistic worship just as he was at the Last Supper for his friends on the night before he died. Hear, too, an echo of the many Scriptures that depict eternal life as a wedding banquet or marriage feast. Two examples are the parable of the wise and the foolish virgins (Matthew 25:1-13) and Isaiah's vision, "On this mountain the Lord of hosts will make for all peoples a feast of rich food, a feast of well-matured wines, of rich food filled with marrow, of well-matured wines strained clear" (Isaiah 25:6).

Much more than host, though. Christ really is the feast himself because the meal is his body and blood shed for us. He only becomes the feast through his willing sacrifice on the cross —once for all. "He it is who gave himself for us that he might redeem us from all iniquity and purify for himself a people of his own who are zealous for good deeds" (Titus 2:14).

> At the Lamb's high feast we sing
> praise to our victorious King,
> who hath washed us in the tide
> flowing from his pierced side;
> praise we him, whose love divine
> gives his sacred Blood for wine,

gives his Body for the feast,

Christ the victim, Christ the priest.[14]

Using the image of the priest's ancient role as one who offers sacrifices to God, this wonderful hymn reminds us that in his self-sacrifice, Christ is victim and priest at the same time. As God, Jesus was the one who instituted the sacrifice; as the Lamb, he was the offering, too. Our Trinitarian theology allows both these mystical things to be True, with a capital "T".

The Mystical Supper[15]
By Sally Brower

In the alchemy of blood and silver,

in the mixture of wine and gold,

we become partakers of divine fire,

full sharers in God's supper of desire.

This is the great banquet of God,

in which we are united,

the lover with the Beloved,

the perfect union imparting life.

This is the feasting on gifts most holy;

this is the meal of love poured out.

This is the mystical moment,

while empty, we become full,

while dying, we rise to new life.

This is the mystical supper

where we become the love we drink.

---

14. The Episcopal Church, *Hymnal 1982* (New York: Church Hymnal Corp., 1982), #174.

15. Unpublished poem by Sally Brower. All rights reserved.

CHAPTER 2

CHALICES

Archaeology tells us that the chalices of early Christians primarily were of glass, though some were of ivory, wood, clay, and occasionally base and precious metals.

Early on, for their daily communion, bishops and priests used a different kind of chalice made from simple materials and shaped like those we have today. In the eucharist, they offered the laity (when they received, usually only at Easter and other high holy days) another type—the *calices ministeriales*. These very large chalices were designed to be seen from the back of churches and often had handles, such as this late fifth- or early sixth-century chalice (see photo overleaf).

Writing in the early 1900s, Roman Catholic historian Herbert Thurston, SJ, observed that the handles "would have afforded additional security against accidents when the sacred vessel was put to the lips of each communicant in turn. In a rude and barbarous age the practical difficulties of Communion under species of wine must have been considerable."[1]

---

1. Herbert Thurston, "Chalice," in *The Catholic Encyclopedia*, vol. III, ed. Kevin Knight (New York: Robert Appleton Co., 1908). *http://www.newadvent.org/cathen/03561a.htm.*

A very large chalice with handles found near *Gourdon*, France. (Wikipedia Commons)

Another ministerial vessel, the Chalice of Ardagh, discovered in 1868 in County Limerick, Ireland, is one of the most beautiful ever found. Seven inches high and nearly 9.5 inches in diameter, the bowl holds three pints! This cup, made from more than 250 main components, is silver alloyed with copper, and it is decorated with gold filigree, multicolored enamels, a large rock-crystal, amber, and malachite.[2]

Inscription of names of twelve disciples helps date Ardagh Chalice to eighth century. (National Museum of Ireland; Wikipedia Commons)

From the year 700 onward, much church legislation dealt with defining the proper materials for chalices and patens. It rejected simple wood chalices because their porous nature could trap the consecrated blood of Christ and never be totally cleansed. Cups made of horn, likewise, were not suitable because they were contaminated in their construction by the blood of the animal to which they originally belonged.

2. "The Ardagh Chalice," The National Museum of Ireland, accessed December 28, 2011, *http://www.museum.ie/en/list/artefacts.aspx?article=bfcd87b3-c3b1-489c-84f3-5c8bc08cc471*.

Later decrees went further, insisting that the paten and chalice be gold, or at least entirely of silver, or pewter for use with the poor. Brass and copper were forbidden because of the possibility of verdigris. Glass was ruled out, too, at one time.

"In the early ages of the Church, the priests were of gold and the chalices of wood, but now the chalices are of gold and the priests of wood."
Attributed to St. Boniface (c. 740) [3]

Still later, the canons directed that the inside of bowls of silver chalices be gilded or given a gold wash. The bowls of pewter vessels, still permitted in "circumstances of great poverty or in time of persecution," also were to be gilded.[4]

The design and workmanship of communion vessels became a high art. Many cups survive and are on display in cathedrals in the British Isles, Europe, and Asia Minor. Many cups still survive as testaments to the devotion of the patrons who commissioned them and the artists who crafted their visions in the most precious metals and gems the earth has to give.

Since 2003 the Roman Catholic Church has allowed dioceses in the United States to use "other solid materials that, according to the common estimation in each region, are precious, for example, ebony or other hard woods, provided that such materials are suited to sacred use and do not easily break or deteriorate."[5]

---

3. Thurston, "Chalice".
4. Ibid.
5. *General Instruction of the Roman Missal (Third Typical Edition)*, trans. International Committee on English in the Liturgy (Washington, DC: United States Catholic Conference, 2003), Sec. 329.

Agate, gold and semi-precious stones enhance eleventh-century Chalice of Doña Urraca at San Isidoro de León in Spain. (By Locutus Borg [José-Manuel Benito Álvarez] [Own work] [CC-BY-SA-3.0 (*www.creativecommons.org/licenses/by-sa/3.0*)], via Wikimedia Commons)

Though The Episcopal Church has no canons dealing with the materials used to create our altar ware, our congregations take great pains to see that their chalices and other communion vessels are beautiful, well-polished, and suitable to the reverence of the occasion. In keeping with centuries of tradition, we still memorialize loved ones with gifts of wonderful artistry to be used in the eucharist.

▩ WHAT IS A KNOP?

The chalice is made of four parts: the bowl, the stem, the base, and the knob. That knob on the stem of many chalices is also called a "knop" or a "nodus" or a "pommellum." It was added to many cups to make them easier for the clergy to handle, particularly when the celebrant raises the chalice during the elevation at the eucharist.

This part of the chalice, often embellished with precious gems, became very prominent during the Middle Ages.

The King James Version of the Bible uses the word "knop" when describing the sacred lampstand crafted to stand before the Ark of the Covenant:

> Three bowls made after the fashion of almonds in one branch, a knop and a flower; and three bowls made like almonds in another branch, a knop and a flower: so throughout the six branches going out of the candlestick." (Exodus 37:19)

▩ DEDICATING A CHALICE

In Anglican theology, church ornaments and furnishings—vestments, stained glass windows, altar cloths, crosses, service books, etc.—"are consecrated by being put to the use for which they were intended"[6] and do not technically need to be blessed, consecrated, hallowed, or otherwise dedicated.

---

6. The Episcopal Church, *The Book of Occasional Services 2003* (New York: Church Publishing, 2003), 196. Hereafter referred to as *BOS*.

Knop design featuring church windows makes it hard for EM to hold. By Unknown from Poland Unknown (muzeumutracone.pl The Lost Museum [Public domain or Public domain], via Wikimedia Commons)

Nevertheless, Episcopalians love their liturgy, and thus The Episcopal Church provides rites for the "Dedicating of Church Furnishings and Ornaments" in *The Book of Occasional Services 2003* (*BOS*, pp. 196–213). The rites provide for a liturgical dedication of the above-mentioned items and more. Any priest may bless them at any time. By ancient tradition, though, the blessing of some church objects is reserved to the bishop—baptismal font, altar, bells, and chalice and paten.

Here is what the bishop prays over the chalice and paten:

Almighty God, whose blessed Son instituted the Sacrament of his Body and Blood: Grant that all who receive the holy Mysteries from these *vessels*, which we now consecrate for use in your Church, may be sustained by his presence and enjoy for ever his heavenly benediction; who lives and reigns in glory everlasting. *Amen.*" (*BOS*, p. 201)

Most old prayers for the setting aside of chalices ask the Holy Spirit to protect the vessels from misuse. In an Anglican prayer from the seventeenth century, the clergyman asks for extra protection in the form of a curse, "And let the curse of this sacred altar, and the curse of my Lord and Master Jesus Xt, bee upon that man, or that woman, that shall purloyne them away, alienate them, or either of them, from their sacred use."[7]

In centuries past, bishops traced a cross using chrism—holy oil—on the paten and then smeared oil over the entire plate. The bishop similarly blessed the chalice, making the sign of the cross in holy oil from rim to rim down through the cup.

If the chalice were misused, broken, or perforated—even if its bowl merely needed regilding and it was sent to the silversmith—it would require reconsecration.

◼ WHAT DID THE CUP AT THE LAST SUPPER LOOK LIKE?

No one knows exactly what sort of cup Jesus passed around after dinner at the Last Supper with the command that we

---

7. J. Wickham Legg, ed., *English Orders for Consecrating Churches in the Seventeenth Century* (London: Harrison & Sons, 1911), 311.

do likewise always in remembrance of him (1 Corinthians 11:25), but probably it was not made of precious metal and never was set with colorful, multifaceted diamonds or rubies the size of grapes.

Experts surmise that Jesus and his friends had modest dinnerware and perhaps used a bronze, pottery, or wooden cup.

It may have been a tumbler the size of a mint julep cup, or could have been a goblet with a base for stability and a very short stem.

A picture of a cup from Jesus' time. (Photo courtesy Gabriel Vandervort | Ancient Resource, *http://www.ancientresource.com*. Used by permission.)

◼ THE HOLY GRAIL

> "And he did the same with the cup after supper, saying, 'This cup that is poured out for you is the new covenant in my blood.'" (Luke 22:20)

The legend of the cup Jesus and the disciples used at the Last Supper is much older than the medieval term "Holy Grail" itself. Pilgrims who went to Jerusalem in the sixth and seventh centuries believed that the actual vessel was still venerated in the church of the Holy Sepulcher. As if one holy relic weren't enough, that particular cup was said to contain the sponge lifted to Jesus while he was hanging on the cross.

> "At once one of them ran and got a sponge, filled it with sour wine, put it on a stick, and gave it to him to drink." (Matthew 27:48)

Chretien de Troyes' poem "Perceval, le Conte du Graal" ("The Story of the Grail"), written between 1180 and 1191, is the first to tell the romantic tale, whose legend has been added to and speculated upon by writers ever since.

What the "grail" really is is still up for debate. The oldest spelling is "graal," thought to be from words in Old French meaning "a cup or bowl of earth, wood, or metal."[8]

INDIANA JONES

In *Indiana Jones and the Last Crusade*, several characters have to pick the holy grail from among dozens of different cups ranging from bejeweled to plain. The first character

---

8. T.C. Donkin, *An Etymological Dictionary of the Romance Languages: Chiefly from the German of Friedrich Dietz* (London: Williams & Norgate, 1864), 236.

wrongly selects the most ornate bejeweled chalice. Indiana correctly chooses the most simple, saying, "*That's* the cup of a carpenter!"

(Wikipedia Commons)

In his 2003 novel *The Da Vinci Code*, Dan Brown casts Mary Magdalene as the grail, instead of supposing it was a physical drinking vessel from the Last Supper or the one that captured blood and water from Christ's lanced side on the cross. Others have identified the grail as another object, such as the aforementioned spear that pierced Christ's side, or a noncorporeal spiritual power.

Even today, churches vie with one another for the recognition that they are the present-day owners of the grail. The Holy Chalice of Valencia, built around a finely polished dark brown agate cup dating from 100–59 BC, is a leading contender. Its gems, pearls, and golden handles have been added to the original relic over the centuries.

Gerald Warner and Stephen Klimczuk, authors of *Secret Places, Hidden Sanctuaries: Uncovering Mysterious Sights,*

Symbols, and Societies, say, "We take the view that . . . in some sense—every chalice used at a Catholic Mass (or an Orthodox divine liturgy) *is* the Holy Grail, as time and space are rendered obsolete in the mystery of the Eucharist. That would arguably make the original holy cup, should it still exist, no more or less exalted than any other consecrated chalice used around the world today."[9]

■ TYPES OF CHALICES

Our modern chalices are of two basic types: those with wide bowls and those with small mouths and deep bowls. Each of these basic shapes can present challenges.

Wine in the broad-bowl chalice sloshes easily because of the wine's large surface area, but it's easier to gauge the amount of wine in it because you can clearly see down into the bowl. It is very easy, however, for you or a parishioner accidentally to dunk your fingers into the wine at intinction.

By Sigfridus. (Public domain, via Wikimedia Commons. Chalice [Cup] anno 1250 from Borgå Cathedral [Porvoo Cathedral]).

9. Gerald Warner and Stephen Klimczuk, *Secret Places, Hidden Sanctuaries: Uncovering Mysterious Sights, Symbols, and Societies* (New York: Sterling Publishing, 2009), 55.

Narrow chalices (often called tulip-shaped chalices) have narrow openings that can make it difficult for EMs to determine if the congregant has gotten a sip of wine. It's often hard to see the level of wine in the depths of the cup. Chalices of this shape also make intinction difficult, particularly if the wine level is low. Some EMs' fingers will not be long enough to dip the bread. If the wafer or bread falls into this type of chalice, it can be hard to remove. (See page 102 in chapter 7.)

A seventeenth-century engraving of the gold chalice, said to have been made by Saint Eloi for Chelles Abbey in the seventh century. The chalice was lost at the time of the French Revolution when Chelles was dissolved. (Wikipedia Commons)

Chalices that are not well constructed for balance—for instance, those with a small base and large bowl—are easy to knock over.

The Antioch Chalice, first half of sixth century, Metropolitan Museum of Art. (Wikipedia Commons)

Large communion chalices can easily be seen at a distance. (Wikipedia Commons)

Vessel size often varies, too. A dainty cup is difficult to handle at the altar rail, though it works well for home communions. Too large a chalice is just as troublesome for the opposite reasons. The size and formality of a service usually dictate the type of chalice used. From the back row of a crowded church, a large chalice will better be seen on the altar as a symbol of Christ's blood. If the gathering is more intimate and informal, smaller vessels are more appropriate.

Most churches use silver chalices on Sundays. Sterling silver chalices are heavier than silver plated ones, and gold cups are the heaviest (and rarest!) of all. (Most "gold" chalices nowadays are actually brass or some other alloy with gold plating.) The thin rims of vessels forged from precious metals make it easy for communicants' lips to seal around them for a sip. This certainly aids you in your EM duties!

Lips do not seal as tightly around the rims of chalices that are thicker, such as those made of heavily chased metal, pottery, wood, and pewter. Wine is more likely to drip out the sides of mouths, so be ready with your purificator!

Practicing helps the EM develop an instinct for how full the chalice is and how far to tip it to give the communicant the right amount of wine. You should develop a sense of what it feels like to give just enough wine—not too little or too much. Also, observant EMs can pick up clues from the person at the rail to guide them in sensing how much wine is enough.

CHAPTER 3

CANONS AND THEIR HISTORY

Once, only licensed Lay Readers could serve the chalice at communion, and then only when an "insufficient number" of clergy were present at the service.

As the twenty-first century dawned, The Episcopal Church began to understand theologically that Eucharistic Ministers' service at the altar is not a matter of "need," or of "helping" the clergy. Laypeople have an authentic sacramental call representing one of the four orders of ministry—laypeople, bishops, priests, and deacons—and by far the largest order at that!

The Episcopal Church's evolving canons tell the tale of how the denomination has wrestled with the inclusion of laity in the sacramental life of the congregation.

In 1976, General Convention opened the ministry just a bit to laity who were not Lay Readers with Title III, Canon 25.5: "Under special circumstances, a lay person other than a Lay Reader may deliver the cup at the Holy Communion, with the permission of the Bishop."[1]

---

1. *Journal of the General Convention of . . . The Episcopal Church, Minneapolis, 1976* (New York: General Convention, 1977), C-58. *http://www.episcopalarchives.org/cgi-bin/acts/acts_resolution.pl?resolution=1976-C031.*

Notice that this is allowed only "under special circumstances" and with the bishop's permission. Not much of an opening but the first small steps.

Those "special circumstances" for other laity included the same caveat under which Lay Readers served the chalice, cases in which there were not a sufficient number of clergy attending the service. There was as yet no name for this ministry, but the notes from that time mention "chalice bearer."

After affirming and expanding the theology of lay ministries in 1982, but not yet passing a canon for acknowledging them, General Convention 1985 passed a new Title III, Canon 3 designating specific lay ministries for the first time. The ministry we know today as Eucharistic Minister finally gained a name when it was included under a two-pronged canon originally called "Lay Eucharistic Minister." Laypeople were licensed to serve the cup at communion and/or take the body and blood directly from the Sunday service to the sick.

This caused a great deal of confusion at the time, as some bishops insisted that only those who had Lay Reader licenses could train for this ministry. Some also required that the laity be licensed as both types of Lay Eucharistic Ministers whether they felt called to both or not.

For comparison's sake, here is the entire text of that seminal 1985 resolution—Title III, Canon 3:

Sec. 1. A confirmed adult communicant in good standing, committed and prepared to serve the Church as a Lay Eucharistic Minister, may be specially licensed to this extraordinary ministry by the Bishop or Ecclesiastical Authority of the Diocese in which the person is canonically resident.

Sec. 2. Such special license shall be given only at the request, and upon the recommendation, of the Member of the Clergy in charge of the Congregation in which the Lay Eucharistic Minister will be serving. The license shall be issued for a period of time not to exceed three years and shall be revocable at any time by the Bishop, or by the Member of the Clergy at whose request it was granted.

Renewal of such special license shall be determined on the basis of the Lay Eucharistic Minister's acceptable performance of this ministry, and upon the endorsement of the Member of the Clergy in charge of the Congregation in which the person is serving.

Sec. 3. It is clearly understood that such ministry is not to take the place of the ministry of Priests and Deacons in the exercise of their office, and should normally be under the direction of a Deacon of the Congregation, if there be one. Persons so ministered to should also be visited regularly by the clergy of the parish.

Sec. 4. Qualifications, requirements, and guidelines for the selection, training and use of such Lay Eucharistic Ministers shall be established by the Ordinary of the Diocese; Provided, that the functions of the Lay Eucharistic Minister shall be limited to the following:

(a) Administering the Cup at any Celebration of Holy Eucharist if there is an insufficient number of Priests or Deacons present.

(b) Directly following a Celebration of Holy Eucharist on Sunday or other Principal Celebrations, if so authorized by the Member of the Clergy in charge of the Congregation and especially licensed thereto by the Bishop, taking the Sacrament consecrated at the Celebration to those

> members of the congregation who, by reason of illness or
> infirmity, were unable to be present at the Celebration.[2]

Notice that "insufficient number" is in Sec. 4 (a), and only the cup is to be administered by a layperson. In order to make up a sufficient number of clergy, the ordained who were even *attending* were counted. In those days, clergy worshiping in the congregation literally would be asked to assist in serving the eucharist at the altar. This cut down on the number of laity serving at the rail. It also annoyed quite a few ordained people, some of whom were worshiping with their families and others of whom were trying to enjoy retirement!

When the national canons changed again in 1988, laity could serve communion if not enough clergy were present at the *altar* to serve the faithful.

> Sec. 5 (a) (1). Administering the elements at any Celebration
> of Holy Eucharist in the absence of a sufficient number of
> Priests or Deacons assisting the celebrant.[3]

This may sound like a picky point, but in fact it opened the opportunity to many more laity to bear the cup.

The limitation of a sufficient number of clergy was removed by canon in 2000, but many clergy and laypeople still are not aware of that and/or do not agree with it, so they operate under the previous idea of EMs' service being "needed" if not enough priests or deacons are available.

---

2. *Journal of the General Convention of . . . The Episcopal Church, Anaheim, 1985* (New York: General Convention, 1986), 278. *http://www.episcopalarchives. org/cgi-bin/acts/acts_resolution.pl?resolution=1985-B004.*

3. *Journal of the General Convention of . . . The Episcopal Church, Detroit, 1988* (New York: General Convention, 1989), 239. *http://www.episcopalarchives. org/cgi-bin/acts/acts_resolution.pl?resolution=1988-A123.*

In 1997, the term "Lay Eucharistic Visitors" was first used for those licensed under the Lay Eucharistic Minister canon who took the bread and wine out of worship to the ill and infirm. This finally distinguished their call from "Lay Eucharistic Ministers" who administered the chalice at communion.[4]

The General Convention that met in Denver in 2000 passed two resolutions notable in EM history. First, it removed the word "adult" from the phrase "confirmed adult communicant" in Sec. 1 (a). This was done to include younger Episcopalians who increasingly sense a call to licensed lay ministries. The canon now only specifies that a person be confirmed and a communicant of a particular congregation in which she will serve.

The second notable action in Denver paved the way for the form of the EM canon that Episcopalians are familiar with today. The bishops and deputies approved an entire rewrite of the Title III canons on ministry in the interim between conventions.

With the promised rewrite of Title III in 2003, the term "Eucharistic Minister" came into being. The authors of those canons, the Ministry Development Committee of the House of Bishops, dropped the word "lay" from all ministry descriptors in an effort to emphasize a theological point: that all ministry is from the Lord and all is equally valuable to the Body of Christ. The distinction of clergy or lay is not necessary in a ministry title. It was in this rewrite also that EMs were "authorized to administer the Consecrated Elements," meaning that they also could distribute the body as well as the blood.

---

4. *Journal of the General Convention of . . . The Episcopal Church, Philadelphia, 1997* (New York: General Convention, 1998), 279. *http://www.episcopalarchives.org/cgi-bin/acts/acts_resolution.pl?resolution=1997-D045.*

Sec. 6. A Eucharistic Minister is a lay person authorized to administer the Consecrated Elements at a Celebration of Holy Eucharist.[5]

Just as with the "insufficient number" clause, whose deletion from the canon is ignored in many of today's Episcopal Churches, so too is the canonical permission for a licensed EM to distribute the bread. Many clergy, especially, have theological reservations about this change because historically the paten has been reserved to the presider of the eucharist. On the other hand, I have attended worship in which all the ministers serving the body and the blood were laypeople, which is not what the church intends! This theology is just as unsound as when all the ministers of communion were clergy. Much more teaching needs to be done.

The 2003 version of the EM canon is nearly identical to the one EMs operate under today. General Conventions in 2006, 2009, and 2012 made few if any changes.

■ OTHER IMPORTANT CANONICAL INFORMATION

The entire title is impressive:

"Constitution & Canons
Together with the Rules of Order
For the Government of the Protestant Episcopal Church
in the United States of America
Otherwise Known as
The Episcopal Church"

---

5. *Journal of the General Convention of . . . The Episcopal Church, Minneapolis, 2003* (New York: General Convention, 2004), 641–67. *http://www.episcopalarchives.org/cgi-bin/acts/acts_resolution.pl?resolution=2003-A111.*

Title III of those canons is the one that deals with the Ministry of the Church. EMs have their own canon, currently designated Title III, Canon 4, Sec. 6,[6] but this can change when General Conventions add to or subtract from the documents every three years at General Convention.

The first canon in Title III deals with all licensed ministries.

Sec. 1 (a) A confirmed communicant in good standing or, in extraordinary circumstances, subject to guidelines established by the Bishop, a communicant in good standing, may be licensed by the Ecclesiastical Authority to serve as Pastoral Leader, Worship Leader, Preacher, Eucharistic Minister, Eucharistic Visitor, Evangelist, or Catechist. Requirements and guidelines for the selection, training, continuing education, and deployment of such persons, and the duration of licenses shall be established by the Bishop in consultation with the Commission on Ministry.

EMs are represented here as a separate ministry instead of as an adjunct to Eucharistic Visitors, with which they were linked for so long. Here are other important points for EMs:

- You must be a "confirmed" Episcopalian or have been received by the bishop into The Episcopal Church if you were confirmed in another denomination.
- You must be a "communicant" of your congregation, that is, a member who is on the books.
- You must be in "good standing," meaning that you give money regularly to the support of your church's ministry.

---

6. The Episcopal Church, *Constitution and Canons . . . for The Episcopal Church 2009* (New York: Church Publishing, 2010), 65–68. *http://www.episcopalarchives.org/CandC_2009.pdf*. Hereafter referred to as *Constitution and Canons 2009*.

- You must be licensed by the bishop to be an EM.
- You must follow all the "requirements and guidelines for the selection, training, continuing education, and deployment" that your bishop has set down. Not all dioceses require the same things.
- You must keep track of how long you are licensed for and renew in a timely manner, usually by taking more training.

> Sec. 2 (a) The Member of the Clergy or other leader exercising oversight of the congregation or other community of faith may request the Ecclesiastical Authority with jurisdiction to license persons within that congregation or other community of faith to exercise such ministries. The license shall be issued for a period of time to be determined under Canon III.4.1(a) and may be renewed. The license may be revoked by the Ecclesiastical Authority upon request of or upon notice to the Member of the Clergy or other leader exercising oversight of the congregation or other community of faith.

- It is up to your rector or vicar or whoever is in charge of your congregation to ask the bishop to license you to be an EM. You must be recommended by him or her to the bishop.
- If you feel you are called to this licensed ministry, your clergyperson must also see that call in order to recommend you. The ministry of an EM is a call affirmed within a specific community, not a right.
- The clergyperson in charge of your congregation can ask that your license be revoked by the bishop.
- The bishop can revoke your license, with notice to your clergy.

- This is not done lightly, but it is done if the EM is not dependable, does not attend church when he is not serving, is destructive to the life of your community of faith, etc.
- "Other community of faith" refers to camp and conference centers, monasteries, and other places where Episcopal Christians live in community.

> (b) In renewing the license, the Ecclesiastical Authority shall consider the performance of the ministry by the person licensed, continuing education in the licensed area, and the endorsement of the Member of the Clergy or other leader exercising oversight of the congregation or other community of faith in which the person is serving.

- Your license is not automatically renewed.
- This is a list of things that the Bishop considers before renewing it:
  - Your performance in the ministry
  - Continuing education that shows that you are engaged with your faith
  - Your clergy's endorsement

> (c) A person licensed in any Diocese under the provisions of this Canon may serve in another congregation or other community of faith in the same or another Diocese only at the invitation of the Member of the Clergy or other leader exercising oversight, and with the consent of the Ecclesiastical Authority in whose jurisdiction the service will occur.

- You may not serve as in EM in any congregation or diocese but your own.

- If you want to, perhaps at a wedding or a funeral, you must be invited by the clergy leader in that congregation AND approved by the bishop of that diocese.
- If you change your church membership even within your own diocese, you will have to go through the licensing procedure again. This might mean you will have to take more training.
- It's up to the bishop to decide if he or she will license you in your new parish and what the procedures are to obtain that license.
- Your new clergy leader also must recommend you to be licensed in your new congregation. This is not a given, so you might want to speak with her before you move. It is entirely possible that she will want to get to know you first as a parishioner before she will commit to recommend you.

> Sec. 6. A Eucharistic Minister is a lay person authorized to administer the Consecrated Elements at a Celebration of Holy Eucharist. A Eucharistic Minister should normally act under the direction of a Deacon, if any, or otherwise, the Member of the Clergy or other leader exercising oversight of the congregation or other community of faith.

- You are licensed to administer both the bread and the wine, so if someone suddenly hands you a paten, it is all right to administer the body.
- As your spiritual leader, your clergy leader chooses whether EMs serve the bread in your congregation. This is not up for a vote.
- As your spiritual leader, your clergy leader also decides how many EMs serve in any given eucharist and sometimes who will serve.

- As your spiritual leader, your clergy leader also decides how many EMs will be licensed in his parish, unless the bishop has set a limit.
- If you have a deacon, he or she will "normally" run the parish program for EMs. "Normally" does not mean "always." Again, this is up to your clergy leader.
- You will have clergy oversight, which is very important. Remain familiar with parish and diocesan regulations and customs for EMs.

CHAPTER 4

SACRAMENTAL THEOLOGY

A sacrament is "an outward and visible sign of an inward and spiritual grace given unto us; ordained by Christ himself, as a means whereby we receive the same, and a pledge to assure us thereof."[1]

I still can recite that definition, which I had to memorize from the 1928 *Book of Common Prayer* before I was confirmed in 1966. I had no idea then what it meant, and I still think it is confusing, even though I understand it better now after forty plus years. The compilers of the 1979 BCP tried to clarify and modernize the language by saying that the sacraments are "outward and visible signs of inward and spiritual grace, given by Christ as sure and certain means by which we receive that grace" (1928 BCP, p. 857).

St. Augustine was famously succinct when he defined a sacrament as a sign of a sacred thing.[2] I like Frederick

---

1. The Episcopal Church, *The Book of Common Prayer and Administration of the Sacraments and Other Rites and Ceremonies of the Church According to the Use of The Protestant Episcopal Church in the United States of America* (New York: The Church Pension Fund, 1928), 581. Hereafter referred to as 1928 BCP.

2. Augustin of Hippo, "Letter 138" 1:7, in *Nicene and Post-Nicene Fathers of the Christian Church*, Series I, vol. I, ed. Philip Schaff, trans. Marcus Dods (Edinburgh: T&T Clark, 1886) 1042. *http://www.ccel.org/ccel/schaff/npnf101.pdf.*

Buechner's definition best: "A sacrament is when something holy happens. It is transparent time, time which you can see through to something deep inside time."[3] Eucharistic Ministers are by nature sacramental ministers. So it's important that EMs master some crucial truths about sacraments.

"OF THE UNWORTHINESS OF THE MINISTERS . . ."

Have you wondered whether the state of the bishop's or priest's character, morals, personality, or the state of his or her soul could affect the validness of the sacrament of the eucharist? Have you as an EM ever wondered whether the state of your own soul could affect the sanctity of the cup of Christ's blood you are offering? This is not to imply that the state of all of our souls is not important! Though we try our hardest to keep our spiritual lives healthy, the church recognizes that "all have sinned and fall short of the glory of God" (Romans 3:23).

The church has wrestled with this puzzle since its beginning. St. Thomas Aquinas worked it out in his masterpiece *Summa Theologica* in the thirteenth century (III, 64).

The Anglican Church adopted nearly the same theology. This doctrine is printed in the back of the 1979 BCP in one of the historical documents. Titled "Of the Unworthiness of the Ministers, which hinders not the effect of the Sacraments," Article XXVI of the Articles of Religion explains:

> Although in the visible Church the evil be ever mingled with
> the good, and sometimes the evil have chief authority in

---

3. Frederick Buechner, *Wishful Thinking: A Theological ABC* (New York: Harper & Row, 1973), 82.

the Ministration of the Word and Sacraments, yet foras-
much as they do not the same in their own name, but in
Christ's, and do minister by his commission and authority,
we may use their Ministry, both in hearing the Word of
God, and in receiving the Sacraments. Neither is the effect
of Christ's ordinance taken away by their wickedness, nor
the grace of God's gifts diminished from such as by faith,
and rightly, do receive the Sacraments ministered unto
them, which be effectual, because of Christ's institution
and promise, although they be ministered by evil men"
(BCP, p. 873).

God acts just as fully through one human being as
another.

Sacraments are, indeed, signs, but they are much more.
For example, the water, oil, bread, and wine, and so forth
represent to us baptism, unction, and the eucharist. For
Christians, these everyday, earthly substances are tied to and
also represent heavenly moments: washing away of sins, the
promise of healing, food for eternal life.

But because God instituted these signs, they don't just
symbolize but actually do something: They cause God's
grace to happen in our hearts.

That grace is multidimensional, pointing at the same
time to what God has done in the past, what God is doing
in the present, and what God has promised for the future.
Simultaneously, a sacrament is intensely personal for each
one of us, shares the same meaning for many of us, and
manifests a general meaning for the church as a whole. [4]

---

4. Joseph Martons, "What Are Sacraments?" *Catholic Update*, n.d. *http://www.
americancatholic.org/newsletters/cu/ac0895.asp.*

Finally, no human being, no formula, no earthly matter, cause a sacrament's actions. It is Christ who baptizes, not the priest or the bishop. It is Christ who acts in order to communicate the grace that each sacrament signifies. As St. Augustine explains, the action of the minister performing the sacrament is distinguished from the action of Christ, who acts by his own power. The minister acts by his ministry given to him by Christ. Therefore, "those whom Judas baptized, Christ baptized. In like manner, then, they whom a drunkard baptized, those whom a murderer baptized, those whom an adulterer baptized, if it was the Baptism of Christ, were baptized by Christ."[5]

■ LAITY

Our English word *lay* comes from the Anglo-French *lai*, which itself comes from the Latin *laicus*, which derives from the Greek *laikos,* meaning "of the people," and whose root is *laos*, "the people at large."

As Christians, we use the word *laity* for all baptized people who are not clergy (bishops, priests, and deacons), though the word technically refers to everyone who is baptized.

As far back as the First Epistle of Clement (circa AD 96), the church has divided its ministry into four "orders" or degrees: bishops, priests, deacons, and laypersons. The arrangement of this list says a lot about the importance of each order within the church. "Bishops" historically are named first. But in the 1979 BCP, the sequence was upended when "laypersons" led the list.

---

5. Augustine of Hippo, "Lectures or Tractates on the Gospel of John" 5:18, in *Nicene and Post-Nicene Fathers of the Christian Church*, Series I, vol. VII, ed. Philip Schaff, trans. John Gibb and James Innes (Edinburgh: T&T Clark, 1888) 57. *http://www.ccel.org/ccel/schaff/npnf107.pdf*.

Q: Who are the ministers of the Church?

A: The ministers of the Church are lay persons, bishops, priests, and deacons. (BCP, p. 855)

In rewriting the catechism, the framers of the 1979 book changed this order intentionally, building upon the liturgical renewal movement in which the Roman Catholic Church's Second Vatican Council played an integral part (1962–65). Our Roman Catholic brothers and sisters have done much to help Christianity recapture the importance of all ministers in the church.

In The Episcopal Church, the 1979 edition of our prayer book became the first in Anglicanism to include in its catechism questions and answers about lay ministry.

As well, the 1979 BCP finally gives us a clear and more-than-complete idea of the particular ministries of laypersons.

Q: What is the ministry of the laity?

A: The ministry of lay persons is to represent Christ and his Church; to bear witness to him wherever they may be; and, according to the gifts given them, to carry on Christ's work of reconciliation in the world; and to take their place in the life, worship, and governance of the Church. (BCP, p. 855)

Clearly the days are gone in which ministry belongs to the clergy, professionals hired to do it because laypeople don't have the time! Theologian Caroline Westerhoff recognizes this truth in her book *Calling: A Song for the Baptized:*

[T]he ministers in the eucharistic community are those who are to carry out its mission of reconciliation and restoration, of reuniting the fractured people of the earth with each other and with God. These ministers are the church's laity, bishops, priests, and deacons, and to each is given a particular charge. . . .[6]

With the 1979 BCP, the church recovered an ancient truth: that laypeople are full and equal members of Christ's Body. And with that, laity are re-called to responsibility for the life of the community as well as for their own individual souls.

The institutional Church itself, based on clericalism for so long, has struggled to alter its ways to witness to that truth. Hard-won changes have been long in coming, but once again, the church is welcoming all orders to sacramental ministries, including yours as an EM!

Speaking particularly of the expanded roles of laity in administration of the eucharist, EMs' regular participation in all our communion services bear witness to the eternal truth that the bread and wine do not belong to the clergy. Jesus' blood was shed for all.

For Westerhoff, "each of the four orders of ministers has different functions to perform for the church, the body of Christ, and each is dependent upon the others to make up the whole. . . . [E]ach order is a symbol for the others of what they are and what they are to be."[7]

In a very real way, St. Paul was right! All orders—all people—are joined together in the Body. Only together can we be complete. All reflect upon the others. The ordained are not separate from the laity. All are *laos* because all are first baptized. Recapturing this larger truth that baptism is

6. Caroline A. Westerhoff, *Calling: A Song for the Baptized* (Harrisburg, PA: Seabury Classics, 2005), 15.
7. Ibid.

the first and great sacrament requires re-examining how we live out our theology inside and outside the church.

"Baptism and its call to serve God and the world are Christian identity; specific roles express that identity in accordance with God's calling to each of us to use our unique gifts in service to God's kingdom," say the authors of "Toward a Theology of Ministry," whose document written for General Convention 2000 described their groundbreaking work in defining "ministry" for the new millennium.[8]

How does this equality before God in baptism square with our long-cherished polity? The church still consecrates some people for sacramental tasks in its ordinations of bishops, priests, and deacons. How can we be equal if some of the *laos* are ordained?

Those who wrote "Toward a Theology of Ministry" suggest a typically Anglican *via media*. "In the spirit of Anglican tradition, we strongly affirm a theological both-and: first, God calls all baptized persons to be agents of the kingdom and missioners of God's reconciling love in Christ; and second, God also calls some people within the *laos* to serve Christ's body, the mission community, in particular ways," says the document. "Among these are the ordained, who share an indispensable call to faithful leadership in the *laos* on behalf of God's mission."[9]

We are consecrated in our baptism first, when we were claimed as "Christ's own for ever" (BCP, p. 308). The paper

8. Standing Commission on Ministry Development, Task Group on the Theology of Baptismal and Ordained Ministry, "Toward a Theology of Ministry," Archives of the Episcopal Church, 2000, 12. *http://archive.episcopalchurch.org/documents/Toward_a_Theology_of_Ministry.pdf*.
9. Ibid., 19.

calls baptism "the crux of Christian identity; it establishes the community of disciples."[10]

It is from baptism that laity and clergy get their commission from Jesus to "go therefore and make disciples of all nations, baptizing them in the name of the Father and of the Son and of the Holy Spirit, and teaching them to obey everything that I have commanded you" (Matthew 28:19–20).

Presiding Bishop Katharine Jefferts Schori states:

> Ministry grows out of the Body of Christ. We may not agree on the language to use in talking about that Ministry—we hear terms like total ministry, mutual ministry, and ministry of all the baptized, but all ministry is grounded in baptism. If it's going to be effective ministry, it has to recognize the connectedness of that Body, and express that awareness of collaboration.[11]

She reminds us of something we too often forget. She points out that though EMs are called to fulfill this ministry at the altar rail, neither the ministry of the congregation who receives, nor the ministry of the Eucharistic Ministers who offer ends there. In fact, each eucharist is only a rest stop on our journey that extends far outside the doors of the church. The blessing, taking, breaking, and giving of holy food provides sustenance to God's people for their lifelong journey.

"We need people who know how to give themselves and their ministries away," the Presiding Bishop writes in *A Wing and a Prayer*:

---

10. Ibid., 11.
11. Katharine Jefferts Schori, *A Wing and a Prayer: A Message of Faith and Hope* (Harrisburg, PA: Morehouse, 2007), 23.

There's an old theological term, *kenosis*, that means emptying. It's most often used in reference to God becoming human. If we are made in the image of God, it should characterize our being as well. Our ministry needs to be kenotic. The ordained are called to be icons, models, but not the primary doers of ministry! Our job (as ordained people) is to equip the saints, to provide formation, education, guidance, support, and then to get out of the way.[12]

The concept of emptying, of *kenosis*, adds even more layers to the symbolism we find in the chalice borne by EMs— the cup that empties as God's people drink. "Jesus said to them, 'This is my blood of the covenant, which is poured out for many'" (Mark 14:24). Christ serves us and saves us by pouring himself out, by emptying himself; as EMs we serve God's people as they empty the cup, whose contents save them. It is in Jesus' self-emptying that the cup that we are privileged to share becomes the cup of salvation.

■ WHO AM I?

When you serve as an EM, you are not representing yourself at the altar. You serve as a representative of the *laos*, the people of God. The changes in the 1979 BCP recapture the earliest Christian theology that includes all orders of ministry in the sacramental life of the congregation. The changes The Episcopal Church has made since the 1970s show this clear theological understanding: It is important for all orders of ministry to be at the altar.

---

12. Ibid.

> "The table was not of silver, the chalice was not of gold
> in which Christ gave His blood to His disciples to drink,
> and yet everything there was precious and truly fit to
> inspire awe." —St. Chrysostom [13]

This certainly is true of EMs serving each Sunday. But EMs also are called upon to serve at weddings and funerals, not because there are not enough clergy to distribute the sacrament but because of the symbolic nature of all of God's people worshiping God together around God's holy table—a preview of the heavenly banquet.

As the "Customary for the Episcopal Diocese of Vermont" so eloquently puts it:

> Eucharistic Ministers embody the ministry of all the baptized as they offer the hospitality of God's Table, where the people of God share the benefits of the Paschal sacrifice and renew the new covenant made with us once and for all. In giving food and drink, they symbolize the bond of charity in which Christ calls us as his friends to the banquet of heaven.[14]

---

13. John Chrysostom, "Homilies on the Gospel of Matthew" I:10, in *Nicene and Post-Nicene Fathers of the Christian Church*, Series I, vol. X, ed. Philip Schaff, trans. George Prevost, rev. M.B. Riddle (Edinburgh: T&T Clark, 1888) 22. *http://www.ccel.org/ccel/schaff/npnf110.pdf*.

14. Christian Formation Committee of the Diocesan Commission on Ministry, *Liturgical Ministries Profiles: A Customary for The Episcopal Diocese Of Vermont*, 2006, 15. *http://www.dioceseofvermont.org/Resources/COM/LiturgicalMinProfiles.pdf*.

■ LAITY AND THE SACRAMENTS

Most lay folks may not think of themselves as sacramental people, and most Episcopalians would say, "That's what priests do!" But as a layperson, you are empowered to offer some of our sacraments under certain conditions.

Anglicans recognize seven sacraments, two major and five minor. The major sacraments are those instituted by Christ during his lifetime: baptism and the eucharist. The so-called minor sacraments are holy matrimony, unction of the sick, reconciliation of a penitent, confirmation, and ordination.

From its beginning, the church authorized laypeople to baptize, anoint the sick, and hear confession in emergencies. Depending upon the laws of the individual states, a layperson may even marry people, although the church would consider such a ceremony to be a civil marriage rather than holy matrimony.

If laity do perform any of the above sacraments, the church does not give them the power or authority to bless, so in some sense their action is not "complete." In such cases where laypeople perform a sacrament during an emergency, the clergy later "solemnize" the sacrament by: 1) marking the sign of the cross on the candidate's forehead in baptism; 2) completing the nuptial blessing and blessing the rings of a civil marriage; and 3) pronouncing the absolution in the rite of reconciliation.

Baptism—Any baptized person can baptize in an emergency provided that she uses water and the Trinitarian formula—"I baptize you in the Name of the Father, and of the Son, and of the Holy Spirit" (BCP, p. 307). A layperson does not make the sign of the cross on the candidate's forehead, however, which is a liturgical action reserved to a priest or a bishop.

"If the baptized person recovers, the Baptism should be recognized at a public celebration of the Sacrament with a bishop or priest presiding, and the person baptized under emergency conditions, together with the sponsors or godparents, taking part in everything except the administration of the water" (BCP, p. 314).

I have been greatly blessed to be present at emergency baptisms in hospitals, usually with premature or very sick infants at death's door. The rubrics quoted above begin, "If the baptized person recovers. . . ." There are few thrills that can match welcoming a child who has undergone emergency baptism back into the flock whole and healthy. When the infant is finally brought before God in her congregation, the memory of that heartbreaking time in the neonatal unit points dramatically to the loving, healing God that we worship. It is a moment that the family members often hope for but may never think they would have, and it is both appropriate and moving for the entire church to celebrate it publicly.

Marriage—If a layperson officiates at a marriage, the church considers that marriage to be a civil marriage rather than holy matrimony because only a priest or a bishop can perform the necessary blessing of the union. Theologically, the bride and groom are the ministers of this sacrament because they are the ones making the contract. That contract becomes a sacrament only if it is blessed (BCP, p. 433).

Unction of the Sick—With the 1979 BCP, The Episcopal Church has resurrected the once-common practice of laypeople anointing the sick. "In cases of necessity, a deacon or layperson may perform the anointing, using oil blessed by a bishop or priest"(BCP, p. 456). In some places, laypeople anoint others for healing weekly, perhaps at a side altar during eucharist. Others define "necessity" more strictly, for example:

- The anointing is not a repeated practice with the sick individual,
- The sick individual is in great distress and a priest is not available, or
- The individual is facing a particular procedure, and a priest is not available.[15]

Reconciliation of a Penitent—A layperson can hear confession using the rite of reconciliation. Rather than pronounce absolution, as a priest or bishop would, he prays a general prayer of forgiveness: "Our Lord Jesus Christ, who offered himself to be sacrificed for us to the Father, forgives your sins by the grace of the Holy Spirit" (BCP, pp. 448, 452).

Only those who have been ordained to the priesthood or episcopate (bishops) can celebrate the eucharist in the Anglican Church. Confirmation and ordination are the other sacraments, and they are reserved solely for bishops.

A layperson, specifically a Lay Reader, may preside at the burial of the dead "if the services of a priest cannot be obtained," but burial is not considered a sacrament of the Anglican Church (BCP, p. 490).

---

15. Episcopal Diocese of Arkansas, *Guidelines on Ministration to the Sick in the Episcopal Church in Arkansas,* revised April 29, 2008, 1. *http://episcopalarkansas.org/wp-content/uploads/2010/06/Ministry-to-the-sick-guidelines.pdf.*

CHAPTER 5

DECENTLY
AND IN ORDER

"But all things should be done decently and in order."
1 Corinthians 14:40

If you have been a Eucharistic Minister or watched one, you understand that an infinite number of things can happen unexpectedly. This chapter will help the EM prevent or handle many pitfalls.

First, some guiding principles:

■ REVERENCE AND DIGNITY

"O worship the Lord in the beauty of holiness . . ."
Psalm 96:9, KJV

The rector of my childhood began each service from the rear of the church with this verse from Psalm 96. EMs have a blessed opportunity to help create this "beauty of holiness" for the entire congregation each time you serve. Your demeanor during the liturgy should be reverent and dignified. Match your own pace to that of the presider and to the formality of the occasion. Be unhurried and efficient, but not mechanical. When (not if!) you make a mistake, quietly do what you need to minimize it. Speak in a whisper, if you must speak.

> *Tip:* Pretend you know what you are doing even if you really don't. Most congregants won't notice any mistakes.

■ PRACTICE AND PREPARATION

To broadly paraphrase an Arabic proverb: "Trust in God, but tie up your camel" or a less-colorful English saying, "God helps those who help themselves." The more you practice and prepare, the more comfortable you feel when serving and when responding to the unexpected. Here are a few suggestions:

1. Get the feel of and practice with the different chalices your parish uses.
2. Stay aware of the liturgical rotation for EMs so that you do not forget, miss your assignment, remember at the last minute, or get caught unawares when you arrive to attend church.
3. Seek out continuing education opportunities for EMs in your diocese and elsewhere.
4. Keep up with books, articles, blogs, and websites that discuss the ministry of EMs.
5. Talk with other EMs about your experiences and questions, and problem-solve together.
6. Finally, and most importantly, be diligent about your spiritual life and preparation.

Keep the prayer used at the "Commissioning for Lay Ministries in the Church" in your heart and mind:

Grant, Almighty God, that those who minister the Bread of Life and the cup of blessing may live in love and holiness, according to your commandment, and at the last come to the joy of your heavenly feast with all your saints in light; through Jesus Christ our Lord. *Amen.*[1]

▪ FOCUS AND AWARENESS

It's very easy to lose focus with an ever-flowing stream of congregants coming to the altar rail. Large services take a lot of an EM's energy. Offering the cup can become rote and repetitive. It's practically a law of nature that the minute an EM loses focus, something untoward happens. Focus and awareness are spiritual disciplines as much as anything. Some EMs find it helpful to focus on the fact that each person at the altar rail is a child of God. Strain to see each person as you imagine God sees her.

A STRONG WORD ABOUT CELL PHONES

Turn off your cell phone before the service! Don't merely silence it—turn it off! Under no circumstances should you use or even check your phone during a service while you are an EM. In fact, it is best to leave your cell phone in a secure place and not take it into the eucharist with you at all, even if it is off. (This advice is based on the "lead us not into temptation" principle.)

For EMs who habitually check their phones, this discipline can be challenging. You might be tempted to take the phone into the service in your pocket and leave it on vibrate. Who will be the wiser? Again, remember that even this will

---

1. *BOS*, 190.

draw your focus from the worship of our Lord. I have heard EMs argue that they might need a cell phone in case of an emergency during the service. Churches have land lines, and their sacristies and vestries often have extensions. Plenty of people present will have their phones with them and can dial 911 if it becomes necessary. If you are waiting for an emergency call or text, you should not be serving as an EM; your mind will not be fully on your ministry and on the liturgy. Please . . . find a substitute and let the appropriate people know.

Being an EM at the altar rail is a lot like driving: You must maintain a constant awareness of what is going on around you. Where are the presider, the deacon, the acolytes? What are the other EMs doing at any given time? Did the paten bearer just give bread to that little boy? Do I need a clean purificator? How empty is my chalice, and when and where should I get more wine? Will I have enough in the cup—but not too much—to commune the last few people? Am I being careful on the chancel steps as I go up and down? How close am I to the paten bearer with whom I am paired? Will I have to go into the congregation to commune a parishioner who cannot come forward? Am I keeping up with the traffic flow?

■ COMMON SENSE AND FLEXIBILITY

"Blessed are the pure in heart, for they will see God."
Matthew 5:8

We know that Jesus longs for us to cultivate pure hearts. This means living a life that is pleasing to God out of a single-minded devotion to our Lord. EMs who keep this in mind and heart will make good decisions, both in worship and outside of it. During a service, trust yourself to make the right decisions in the moment. Trust your pure heart, even though it's always a work in progress this side of the kingdom.

If it can happen, it will happen. The moment when "it" happens in the service is not the time for questions or discussion. When "it" happens is the time to deal with the situation calmly, efficiently, and pastorally with a minimum of interruption to the service. You will be able to do exactly that if you are emotionally, physically, and spiritually prepared to be an EM. After the liturgy, analyze the situation and tweak any practices that could have led to or exacerbated it. Blaming someone is not helpful. Liturgical ministers might merely need more practice or a new way of doing something.

Practice never makes perfect . . .

But it helps!

It is crucial for EMs to have experience handling all the different chalices their parish is likely to use. Most churches have an assortment of cups of different heights, weights, materials, and design. Some only pull out the "really good stuff" for Christmas and Easter, so be sure to handle those, too, beforehand. Practice helps EMs develop a feel for the amount of wine left and how far to tip the cup to offer a sip.

I once heard an EM puzzling over how to administer a triangular chalice. "How do I wipe and turn if it's not round?" he asked. Over the years I have encountered gorgeous ornate chalices too bulky for my small hands to wrap around the stem and too heavy for my small wrists. Conversely, a dainty, delicate chalice might be hard for those with larger hands. Practicing ahead of time alerts EMs to similar problems.

The cross-shaped base on the chalice below would make it difficult for a Eucharistic Minister to hold and turn while wiping it.

By Garitzko (Own work) [Public domain], via Wikimedia Commons. The Emperor's chalice in the treasure chamber of the town hall of Osnabrück. Medieval chalice.

At the altar

As a member of the altar party, an EM follows the customs of her parish. Do you kneel for confession? Do you cross yourself and, if so, when? Where are you expected to sit? Do you have other duties in the chancel? Where do you stand during the consecration? Your clergy will instruct you in these practices, which vary from congregation to congregation.

Your role during the prayer of consecration is crucial, helping the mass appear reverent and planned. Match the presider as he crosses himself and when he bows. Learn the liturgical style of your clergy so you will follow each one seamlessly; their practices vary.

Handing off a chalice can be risky business, certainly increasing the opportunities for sloshes and spills. That is why I prefer that EMs take a chalice and purificator from the altar themselves, and if they need to refill it, to set it on the altar to do so, holding it steady there. If an EM is going to switch chalices or give hers to another EM, again it is wise to set it on the altar for the other to take up instead of making a hand-to-hand pass in midair.

However, in some traditions, laypeople do not set anything upon the altar or remove anything from it. In this case, a priest will hand you the chalice and purificator to use at the altar rail instead of gesturing for you to take it from the altar. After the serving of communion, hand your used cup and purificator to a priest or deacon, who will put it in the proper place.

Who receives communion?

The Episcopal Church considers a person's baptism to be valid if she has "received the Sacrament of Holy Baptism with water in the Name of the Father, and of the Son, and of the Holy Spirit, whether in this Church or in another Christian Church. . . ."[2]

Additionally, the church says: "No unbaptized person shall be eligible to receive Holy Communion in this Church."[3]

At the moment, The Episcopal Church is in the midst of a complex theological debate about this canon. Presiders at different Episcopal Churches express differing invitations to communion at their services and in their service bulletins. Some invite "all baptized Christians" and others invite "anyone who wants to partake of the body and blood of Christ." At its simplest level, much of the church's current debate weighs the meaning of baptism as an initiation rite into the Body of Christ against a theology of holy hospitality that welcomes all God's people to the Lord's Table.

An EM does not need to sort this out! Though it has a clear canon regulating the subject, the church does not check a person's baptismal certificate as people come to receive communion. As a general principle for your ministry: If an adult wants communion, offer it to him; if a child wants communion, offer it to her if it is all right with the adult(s) accompanying her at communion.

Ask your rector for guidance about current parish and diocesan practice.

Height matters!

The mechanics of sharing the chalice are mainly about physics. Your height has a lot to do with how you manage the main task of your ministry. You also have to take into account the height of the communicant, as well as whether that person is kneeling or standing.

---

2. *Constitution and Canons 2009*, I.17.1(a), 55.
3. Ibid., I.17.7, 58.

Short EMs have an advantage at the altar rail in being closer to the children they communicate. This is great for those times when the little one wants to grab the chalice and for making an encouraging connection with a curious youngster. But without letting go of the chalice, a short person may find it difficult to communicate even a medium-tall adult who chooses to stand at the rail instead of kneeling. You have to reach up and out because the entire altar rail and kneeler are between you. You may have to very carefully relinquish your hold on the chalice when giving wine to very tall people who are standing.

EMs of medium height probably find the ministry physically easier. Tall adults usually are not too tall to communicate, even if they choose to stand, and you don't have to bend so far to give the cup to children. You will usually find yourself the right height to administer the cup to most kneeling adults.

A tall EM can easily get a sore back during a long service that has many communicants. Bending down to give communion to kneeling children also becomes a strain. It is all right to ask them to stand and/or to stand on the kneeler so that you can better reach them. EMs who are tall often say that serving at a standing communion station is the most comfortable posture.

Ways to receive

The Episcopal Church has several modes of distributing communion. The most common are 1) one element at a time, first the body and then the blood, and 2) by intinction, which is lightly dipping the bread into the wine and consuming both together. Each way has its own variations, and both parishes and communicants have different reasons for preferring one way over the other.

The main practical issues with intinction are these: Who is going to dip the bread, and how to keep fingers out of the wine?

The Episcopal Church in many places allows either the communicant to dip and consume his own wafer (self-intinction) or the EM to take it, dip it, and put it on the person's tongue (intinction). This uncertainty causes confusion at the rail unless your congregation or diocese has a preferred method. Often the communicant gives no sign as to whether you should do it or whether he wants to. But you will know once you try to take the bread from someone who wants to dip it himself! Having the EM dip the bread can avoid a host of accidents over having the communicant do it.

I know a bishop who decreed that the manner of intinction would be the same within the entire diocese: The EMs would dip for communicants and place the bread on their tongues. That certainly made things clear for clergy and EMs. However, not all the laypeople of the diocese knew about the policy or agreed with it. Thus ensued tugs of war at the altar rail with EMs trying to take bread firmly held by communicants bent on self-intinction. Unfortunately, this caused relationship problems between the EMs and parishioners.

One of the reasons some congregants prefer intinction is that they mistakenly believe that it is more sanitary than drinking from the common cup. Science has *not* proven this to be true. One of the problems with keeping the chalice relatively sanitary is that it is difficult to control the depth of the dip. When an EM consistently offers intinction, her training can keep her from letting her own fingers touch the wine. When laity (particularly children) attempt self-intinction, many either do not know to keep their fingers out of the wine in the chalice or that getting their fingers in the wine is unsanitary. Too often, I have seen thoroughly soaked bread grasped by thoroughly soaked fingers emerging from the cup. Tulip-shaped chalices—those with small openings and deep bowls—are notoriously hard to use for intinction, particularly if the level of the wine is low.

Intinction can get particularly messy if the eucharistic bread is not in wafer form but in loaves, because each intinction is liable to leave behind soggy crumbs in the chalice. Speaking as a person who often has to consume what is left in the chalice, this adds a spiritual challenge to the ministry!

■ SANITATION

Recommendations about this important matter are constantly changing. The bottom line for an EM is: Be as clean as you can be.

This includes such practices as:

- Washing your hands with warm soap and water shortly before you go into the service;
- Avoiding touching your hair, face, mouth, eyes, or nose during the service;
- Following recommendations about sneezing into the crook of your arm if you must sneeze. (Even if you have noncontagious allergies, parishioners will notice your wiping your nose and blowing it during the service and assume you are sick.);
- Finding a substitute and not serving if you have a cough, a cold, a fever, or otherwise feel ill. Make that decision early enough before the service so you can get a replacement. When in doubt, err on the side of keeping your germs away from the congregation!

- Using the purificator correctly by wiping both the inside and the outside of the chalice lip with a clean area of the linen after each person drinks, and rotating the edge of chalice between successive communicants;
- Using fortified wine (which has a higher alcohol content) rather than relying on the minor germ-killing properties associated with the silver and gilt of chalices.

Currently, alcohol hand sanitizers are being studied as a health concern, but many parishes now keep them in the sacristy, in the church, and near the altar. If the use of the sanitizers is your parish's practice, maximize the sanitizer's disinfecting power by using it after your own communion and before you take up your chalice.

Some churches are changing the ways that they do things in response to modern health concerns. The Diocese of New York recommends a large enough lavabo to hold soapy water so the priests, deacons, and EMs can wash and rinse their hands thoroughly in the chancel before the eucharistic prayer.[4]

Debate has raged for more a century about how sanitary it is to drink from the common cup. However, according to the Centers for Disease Control, "No documented transmission of any infectious disease has ever been traced to the use of the common cup."[5]

---

4. Mark S. Sisk and Catherine S. Roskam, *Healthcare Concerns and Liturgical Practices: A Memorandum to the Priests and Deacons of the Diocese,* Episcopal Diocese of New York. September 2009. *http://www.dioceseny.org/pages/443-healthcare-concerns-and-liturgical-practices.*

5. Lilia P. Manangan, Lynne M. Sehulster, Linda Chiarello, Dawn N. Simonds, et al., "Risk of Infectious Disease Transmission from a Common Communion Cup," *American Journal of Infection Control* 26, no. 5 (October 1998): 538–39. *http://www.ajicjournal.org/issues?issue_key=S0196-6553%2805%29X7030-4.*

A 1997 study of more than six hundred subjects published in the *Journal of Environmental Health* concluded that "no significant differences were found in the rates of illness among Christians who receive Holy Communion, Christians who attend church but do not receive the sacraments, and people who do not attend Christian services."[6] About one-third of the participants did not attend church at all and the others attended rarely or frequently, with some receiving communion and some not. The methods of reception—intinction, common cup, separate cups—were not specified.

Surprisingly, many studies show that intinction is not a healthier alternative.

Here are some sanitation issues rarely considered with intinction:

- When the EM places the bread into a communicant's hand and the communicant then picks it up for self-intinction, the communicant touches the Host more than if the EM does the intinction, thus introducing more germs into the chalice.
- Intinction by an EM who has sanitized his hands is a much cleaner method for the communicant and for others following after her.
- The most sanitary way to perform intinction is if the EM takes the bread or wafer directly from a paten or ciborium, dips it in the wine, and places it directly into the congregant's mouth.

---

6. Anne LaGrange Loving, et al., "The Effects of Receiving Holy Communion on Health," *Journal of Environmental Health* 60, no. 1 (July/August 1997): 6–10.

If a dangerous virus or bug is going around, bishops will issue guidelines for their churches, much as they did in the 2009 swine flu epidemic.

■ CHALICE TECHNIQUE

"How do I hold the chalice when offering it to a communicant?" is probably the question that EMs ask the most. There are many ways to do this.

The same method does not work for everyone. EMs' hand sizes, strength of grip, and wrist flexibility vary, as do the weights, sizes, and compositions of the chalices EMs routinely use in their parishes. Whether you are left- or right-handed also is a factor.

Experiment to find the best way that works for you with each chalice that you might handle. EMs should gather periodically to practice administering with each chalice, to communicate each other (using water!), and to fit their technique to the individual vessel. Don't forget to practice with the chalices your congregation only uses for special occasions. Often these cups are more ornate and heavier.

I served in a parish that routinely used one chalice that was too heavy for me. If I ended up with that cup during a service, I quietly asked one of the EMs to swap with me. Additionally, I am right-handed but serve the cup with my left!

Like with a backhand stroke in tennis, there are one-handed EM techniques and two-handed EM techniques.

Here are several ways to hold the chalice:

1. Hold the chalice by the knob in the stem between your third and fourth fingers. Some people say this gives a good grip for tipping it toward the communicant's lips.

2. Hold the chalice with two hands, one on the stem and the other one on the bowl itself.

3. Do what works best for you!

If the congregant guides the cup by its base, it is enormously helpful.

With whichever method you use, you will still need a hand to wipe the lip of the chalice with the purificator.

■ A PAEAN TO PURIFICATORS

Altar linens are an essential and beautiful part of our eucharistic worship. They have developed over many centuries, and each is the right shape and size for its purpose. The purificator is a small white cloth that serves myriad functions, most of which involve cleanup. It's an essential tool for EMs, who should be familiar with what it looks like, how to use it, how to handle it, and what to do with it when they are finished with it.

The old saw about using the right tool for the job applies to EMs, too! Working with a linen other than a purificator makes your task harder!

HOW TO IDENTIFY A PURIFICATOR

Here are some clues:

Along with a chalice, EMs are handed a linen or select one from the altar. The purificator should be square and ironed into thirds vertically and horizontally, so that you have nine equal sections folded into one. The embroidered symbol (usually a cross) should be in the middle of the cloth (see first image on page 71).

If by chance you have a rectangular linen of six sections folded in half, it's likely a lavabo towel, the cloth on which the celebrant dries her hands at the ablutions:

If your "purificator" looks too large, the material seems too thin, or the embroidered symbol is along an edge, it's a corporal. This is the square piece set beneath the wine and the bread (see below). (The Body of Christ is placed on a corporal, which is from a Latin word referring to a physical body.)

An EM will find a lavabo towel and a corporal awkward for properly wiping the chalice. The cloths are either too large or the wrong shape.

Tip: It's best to check the purificator when you first take it up, but if you realize later that you have the wrong linen, exchange it for a purificator at your first opportunity if one is available. Altar guild members are the experts on these linens, so ask for a tutorial!

Soiled linens

Purificators are primarily for cleaning the lip of the chalice, so they become dirty easily and quickly. EMs often need to use several during one service, so it's very important to know where the extras are. Most often, additional purificators are in the burse—the fabric-covered "envelope" that tops the veiled chalice and paten at the beginning of the service.

A burse. (Broederhugo from nl [CC-BY-SA-3.0 (*http://creativecommons. org/licenses/by-sa/3.0/)*], *from Wiki-media Commons*)

Some churches keep additional purificators on the credence table. Wherever they are, don't hesitate to get a clean purificator if you need one. Few things are more unattractive and unsettling to a communicant than watching you wipe the lip of the chalice you are about to offer with an obviously soiled purificator.

If you happen to have folded up in your purificator an unsanitary wafer, exchange your purificator for a clean one as soon as you can, as it's easy to drop the wafer out of it while communing others at the rail.

If you need a clean one, refold the soiled purificator and place it on the altar or the credence table as directed. If it's very soggy and messy because of a spill, don't put it directly on top of any other linen on the altar or credence table because it will stain that linen.

Parishes vary in their customs about what their EMs do after everyone has communed. Regardless of whether you consume the wine in your chalice or leave it, usually you will place the chalice and its used purificator on the credence table, draping the soiled, half-folded purificator over the chalice.

Tip: Stuffing the soiled purificator down into the cup can leave a mess when the linen soaks up any extra wine. Altar guild members generally have specific requests about not doing this.

A purificator draped over a chalice. By Paterm (Own work) (GFDL [CC-BY-SA-3.0 (*http://creativecommons.org/licenses/by-sa/3.0/*) or CC-BY-SA-2.5-2.0-1.0 (*http://creativecommons.org/licenses/by-sa/2.5-2.0-1.0*)], via Wikimedia Commons)

Except in an emergency, I do not recommend paper purificators. For one thing, the proper way to dispose of used ones is to burn them!

To unfold or not to unfold

If that helps you do your job better, it's OK to unfold and use the entire purificator. (Except for soiling the embroidery in the center!) If you do unfold the entire cloth, know that you run a greater risk of soaking a large area of it in the wine as you go down the rail, creating a mess. On the other hand, the advantage of this technique is that wiping the lip with a single layer of cloth on both sides cleans it best.

YOUR ALTAR GUILD WILL THANK YOU IF . . .

1. When wiping the cup, stay clear of the embroidery (usually a cross) in the center of the purificator. Wine stains, dirt, and lipstick soak into those threads, making them difficult to clean.

2. When you finish giving communion, drape your used purificator folded in half over the used chalice instead of pushing it down inside the cup, where leftover wine will further stain the linen.

3. Don't leave a used purificator on the altar or the credence table without letting the deacon, a priest, and/or an altar guild member know its status, particularly true if:

   a. The linen is soaked with wine;

   b. The cloth looks clean but is not (e.g., it has been dropped; the stains don't show; it has been used to clean a spill);

   c. Or, consecrated bread is folded up in the purificator. An altar guild member will need to know this before she picks it up and risks dropping the bread out of it.

4. You point out to an altar guild member after the service where any wine was spilled.

5. You want to know anything about cleaning linens that have consecrated wine stains or vessels that have held the bread and wine. The members will be glad to show you how to handle cleaning these holy things.

Many EMs also develop their own purificator folding methods—often intricate ones—that work for them. I prefer to use my purificator folded into thirds, refolding to get a clean surface as necessary.

Here are other important things to know:

- The goal is to keep the lip of the cup as clean as you can. Use an unsoiled part of the purificator every time that you wipe.
- Carefully monitor the linen's cleanliness as you use it.
- Holding the purificator in the opposite hand from the one gripping the chalice usually works best.
- Always wipe after each person takes a sip.
- Rotating the chalice a quarter turn after each communicant who sips, work your way around the lip of the chalice, using the entire bowl. This way, you are changing the spot from which the next communicant will drink after each wipe.
- There is no need to wipe after intinction.

Sometimes an EM can get a surprise on the purificator. An EM tells the story that when he was new to the ministry, he looked down in horror as a dark red bloody streak appeared on the linen after he wiped the lip of the chalice. It turned out to be only lipstick.

How to "wipe and turn"

The "wipe and turn" technique seems to work best for EMs trying to keep the chalice as clean as they can for communicants. This entails wiping both the inside and the outside of the chalice lip, which you easily can do.

Offer the cup and tilt it to help the congregant drink a sip. When you bring the chalice back toward you, firmly pinch its lip on both sides with the purificator in the spot where the person drank. Wipe the lip in one direction at the same time as you twist the stem of the chalice in the opposite direction, rotating the vessel a quarter turn. This action applies a bit of pressure to the spot being cleaned as the purificator moves over it. You don't have to rub hard.

There is no "right" way to hold the purificator when you are wiping the rim as you make your way down the altar rail, but here are two techniques to try:

1. Draping the purificator over your thumb and index finger, pinch the rim of the vessel between the cloth. Unfolding the entire linen helps keep the cloth layers manageable when you are wiping. Work with the middle of the linen and stay away from the corners and edges with this technique because they tend to dangle in the chalice!

2. Draping the purificator over your index finger (or index and middle fingers), cover your palm with the linen. Let it hang free or put the hanging end between your ring and pinky fingers. Form a "groove" between your index and middle fingers to wipe the lip of the chalice.

The antiquated method of looping the purificator over an index finger and wiping the outside of the cup does not clean the inside lip of the chalice.

Tip: Don't wipe too deeply inside the chalice, especially if it is full, or your purificator will soak up the wine.

Tip: Directions can be confusing, but a picture is worth a thousand words. So ask an experienced EM to demonstrate these techniques, and you'll catch on quickly!

■ SENTENCES OF ADMINISTRATION

Ideally, your choice should "match" that of the paten bearer with whom you are paired. You have three choices if you are bearing the cup. All are in the *Prayer Book* and need to be memorized. These are the only sentences allowed by The Episcopal Church. EMs should not add to nor shorten them! EMs have offered me the chalice without saying anything, as well as with an unfamiliar phrase. This should never happen!

The BCP designates three choices for administering the cup in Holy Eucharist Rite I. Only the first choice is in Rite I language, i.e., "thy" and "thee" (and comes from the 1928 BCP), and it seems to be falling out of use even in Rite I.

The Blood of our Lord Jesus Christ, which was given for thee, preserve thy body and soul unto everlasting life. Drink this in remembrance that Christ's Blood was shed for thee, and be thankful. (BCP, p. 338)

If using the long form, I recommend one sentence per communicant, starting the second sentence "Drink this . . ." when reaching the second congregant. In this case, it takes two communicants to get through the whole two sentences of administration. It is theologically all right to split the sentences.

The other two choices for Rite I are also the same as the sentences of administration for Rite II:

> The Blood of our Lord Jesus Christ keep you in everlasting life. [Or]
> The Blood of Christ, the cup of salvation. (BCP, p. 365)

Do not use the above sentences with two communicants, for instance, "The Blood of Christ," to parishioner no. 1 and "the cup of salvation" to parishioner no. 2 kneeling next to her. Doing that sounds as if you are rushing along what should be a precious moment for each one.

Also, do not truncate the BCP words of administration to "the Blood of Christ," saying just the first part of the phrase to each communicant at the altar rail, which is too often done. Both parts are theologically necessary to link the sacrament (Christ's blood) to its effect (salvation).

The same goes for the phrase, "The Blood of our Lord Jesus Christ keep you in everlasting life." In this case, Christ's blood is linked to its effect: everlasting life.

The EM uses the same sentence of administration whether he does intinction or the person does not partake of the wine. If the communicant does not take the cup, hold the chalice out at a little higher level than you would if he were going to drink of it and say the same sentence of administration as if he were drinking the wine. Some may want to reach out and touch the base of the chalice at this time.

> *Tip:* If you suddenly draw a blank and forget the sentence of administration, administer the cup without words until you get back on track.

If for some reason you say the wrong sentence—I have occasionally said, "The Body of Christ . . ." when giving the cup—don't worry about it. Move forward with the correct phrase.

▉ TO LOOK OR NOT TO LOOK

The time during the eucharist when a person receives the body and blood of Christ is a clear sign of joining in communion with those present (and even the "communion of saints" past and future). However, at the same time, the instant is an intimate individual moment between a human being and God, through the gift of Christ and in the Holy Spirit.

EMs privileged to serve at the altar rail face congregants in different spiritual attitudes. Some are more gregarious, gazing into the EM's eyes in thanksgiving for the great gift. In a growing number of communities of faith, people are named as they are given the body and blood, e.g. "Susie, the Blood of Christ, the cup of salvation."

On the other hand, some communicants at the rail are deep within themselves, savoring the moment. Often these people will not look at you, and some have been taught not to. In certain circles, theologians stress the anonymity of the persons distributing the bread and wine, believing that personal contact with the communicant draws attention from our Lord at the most significant moment.

EMs learn to respect those differences and not force someone to look up or avoid the gaze of a person who wants that contact. I find that most children are eager to look the EM in the eyes!

Sometimes it's hard to know what communicants expect. But as you get to know your congregation, you soon will learn individual preferences as communicants come forward to commune with God.

■ HATS

Many challenges await EMs at the altar rail. Take hats, for instance; women's big hats in particular. They are marvelous and often colorful. But their brims can hide a kneeling communicant's entire face, so that you will not be able to see where to offer the chalice. These fashionable ladies rarely look up at the EM. Perhaps they are afraid of tilting their heads back too far and losing their headgear. The EM's best technique is to bend sideways and peek under the hat as you offer the chalice beneath the shelf of the brim. Because you often cannot see her lips, the dangers are these: You withdraw the cup before she has had a sip or you inundate her with wine.

■ CHILDREN

Children can be a delightful challenge for the EM and come along with myriad issues requiring some forethought. If you are not clear about what to do, ask an adult who is with the child. If the youngster is old enough, it's respectful to ask her. This can help children feel included in what is going on at the altar rail.

Nearly universally, here is the main difficulty: Did the child receive the bread? If so, does he receive the wine? This is one of the reasons to keep an eye on the paten bearer, whose action can clue you in as to whether to offer the cup. You might be able to tell when you come near by whether the child reaches for the chalice. This can get messy in a heartbeat. Children are much more likely to grab the chalice suddenly. Also, the adult might grasp the cup unexpectedly, intending to help. Some parents choose to not allow their child to drink the wine. Do not knowingly go against a parent's wishes about whether the child receives the wine, even if the youngster begs you for the cup.

If he is still holding on to his bread, he might not know what to do with it, especially if it is a wafer, which we all can agree does not look very much like the bread at home! He also might be expecting to dip it. Often I point to the wafer and then to my mouth to indicate that the youngster should eat it. If he wants self-intinction, he usually will make his intentions clear, though it is best if the EM dips the bread; often a child dunks his fingers as well as the host into the chalice.

If he is holding on to a wafer and does not want to consume it, the EM may take it back from him or ask a parent to eat it for the child. If you reclaim it, as soon as you can, consume it yourself or fold it into your purificator. When you place your used linen on the altar or credence table, explain to a deacon or priest that it contains a wafer.

Whether the child is kneeling or standing is also a factor for the EM. If you cannot easily reach a kneeling youngster, you may ask her to stand on the floor or even to stand on the kneeling cushion.

If someone is at a rail with an infant, don't automatically think that the baby does not receive the wine. If the child is baptized, she is a full member of Christ's Body, which means she can receive if the parent allows it. To commune an infant, put a drop of wine from the chalice onto your forefinger and set it onto her lips.

I once saw a newly baptized infant smack his lips at his first taste of communion wine. A beatific smile lit his entire face! His sacramental epiphany was a touchstone for those around him to renew their own wonder and joy at what Christ has given to us.

■ DISABLED AND ELDERLY COMMUNICANTS

Some of this advice applies to the elderly or those who are mentally or physically disabled. Often you will need to be helpful to them in ways different from what you are used to. A person sitting in a wheelchair in the congregation will be much lower than someone kneeling at the rail.

A person also might come forward but because of mobility problems not be able to get near enough for you to offer the chalice. (The paten bearer will have the same problem.) If you can get around the altar rail, you may go to where that person is standing or sitting. If you cannot get to her, the usher can ask her to wait until you can get there.

Sometimes when you go out to commune someone in the congregation, you might have to remind him that he needs to consume the bread he is holding. Intinction is helpful in this situation if the communicant will allow it, because it circumvents an attempt to take the chalice from you.

Once an elderly lady in a nursing home surprised me by grabbing the chalice, downing the entire thing and handing it back to me, smacking her lips loudly as she thanked me. Unfortunately, she was the first communicant in a room full of others and left nothing in the cup for anyone else. This was especially disappointing to the nursing home congregation, who, I later realized, all were looking forward to a little nip of wine, and not in a particularly religious way.

■ COMMUNION STATIONS

Communion stations are a way of communicating large groups of people as efficiently and quickly as possible. The size and types of services dictate the number and location of communion stations. A smaller service might have two stations near the chancel. An enormous one might have six or eight or even more spread throughout the church and even going to a remote site because the nave is full.

Each communion station has someone to distribute the bread and one or more EMs with chalices. As an EM, your assignment is to stand to one side of the person with the paten. Two or more EMs assigned to a communion station generally flank the person with the bread. A communicant approaches, receives the host, and moves to one side to the EM for the wine. The next person takes the host and moves to the EM on the other side. This nearly always confuses those present, most of whom seem to take the wine on one side while leaving the other EM with few people to commune.

> *Tip:* You can do one major thing to make your communion station go as smoothly as possible: Remember that the only person who should have a line waiting in front of her is the one holding the paten. To avoid having people waiting for the cup, EMs should stand several steps from the person giving the bread. If communicants have to take a few steps to get to a chalice, this helps move things along. Since these services are usually long and crowded, you surreptitiously can adjust your position to find your optimal distance. Another helpful action might be to covertly motion a person to your side for the wine if he seems hesitant or things are backed up.

Some other challenges for EMs serving wine at communion stations are related to height, traffic flow, and logistics:

The EM's height—This matters more at a communion station than at an altar rail because all communicants are standing; height differences are magnified. If most communicants are adults, a tall EM finds it easier to administer the cup at a communion station. Since I am very short, if I am near the chancel steps, it works well if I stand on the first step as communicants approach me at floor level.

Traffic flow—Despite instructions to the contrary from the presider or those printed in the service bulletin, many people at large worship services seem to choose their own communion station instead of the one to which they are assigned. Or a line at one communion station may be much shorter and draw communicants from other parts of the church. In the interest of time and efficiency, it usually is OK to quietly motion communicants in a longer line to switch to your station if it is less crowded.

Logistics—EMs serving at communion stations far from the altar also need to know how to get more wine or another purificator. With good liturgy planning, a deacon or other designated person should be nearby to refill chalices as the service progresses. If you will have no access to additional wine, quietly return your chalice to the chancel as directed. If you continue to stand at a communion station with an empty cup, that confuses communicants.

> *Tip:* Put a clean purificator in your pocket if you cannot get to the extras at the altar while you are at a communion station. When switching to your clean one, stash your dirty purificator in your pocket while you are serving. Just remember to remove the dirty linen

from your pocket and place it back on the credence table for the altar guild to properly clean off the consecrated wine.

Tip: Such large services take much longer, and you might communicate many more people than you normally do at an altar rail, so wear comfortable shoes!

WHEN SERVING AT A COMMUNION STATION . . .

☐ What vestments should I wear?

☐ Am I wearing dark, close-toed, and comfortable shoes?

☐ Have I turned my cell phone off and left it in a secure place?

☐ Did I use the toilet and wash my hands?

☐ Do I have a clean purificator in my pocket?

☐ Where are my Book of Common Prayer, necessary hymnal(s), and service bulletin?

☐ Should I carry them in procession or put them in my seat ahead of time?

☐ Where is my place in the procession?

☐ Where will I sit during the service?

☐ Where am I to be during the liturgy of the table?

☐ When do I stand and/or kneel?

☐ When and where should I take my own communion after the consecration?

☐ Where is the hand sanitizer in the chancel?

☐ With whom am I paired (paten bearer and other EM) for communion?

☐ Which chalice will I be using?

☐ Where will we be located within the church?

☐ On which side of the paten bearer should I stand?

☐ Which words of administration should I use?

☐ How will I refill my chalice?

☐ Where are the extra purificators?

☐ Will I help commune people in the pews who cannot come forward?

☐ What should I do with my leftover wine and used purificator?

☐ Where should I stand or sit when I am finished?

☐ Do I remain or leave in the procession?

◼ GLUTEN INTOLERANCE

More and more people are coming to our altar rails with celiac disease, an intestinal illness that afflicts at least 1 in 133 Americans. EMs needs to be knowledgeable about the disease because it affects how they administer the cup, as well as how they, the presider, and the paten bearers handle the Body of Christ.

Celiac disease is an incurable allergic condition set off by specific food-grain antigens (gluten) in wheat, rye, and barley (*http://www.celiac.com/*). Most communion bread, such as wafers, pita, and loaf bread is made with one or more of these grains.

Unlike the canon law of the Roman Catholic Church that specifies that the bread in the eucharist has to be from wheat, the canons of The Episcopal Church don't! This gives Episcopalians more leeway to creatively solve the problems that can bar some of our most faithful parishioners from our eucharists.

In order to be inclusive, some congregations now have a separate chalice for gluten-intolerant members. Using a separate chalice takes preparation and planning. Clergy and EMs must know which vessel is for those with CD, so that chalice should be distinct enough from the others to be easily recognizable. Consult with each other before the service about whether people are present who have these special needs and what accommodations the parish is making for them.

Keep the separate chalice covered and away from the bread, because some people are so sensitive that dust from the hosts can drift into the wine and set off a dangerous autoimmune response.

Thankfully, some cases of CD are milder than others, even so this kind of cross-contamination is a big obstacle and danger for sufferers. During communion, people who dip wafers or bread into the wine leave behind small particles of wheat in the chalice. Tiny bits also can enter the wine from someone sipping from the chalice who has just eaten of the body. Even the presider's breaking of the bread over the chalice can contaminate it for those with CD.

Because celiac disease seems to be increasing, some congregations use low-gluten or gluten-free hosts, both of which are easily available online. In other churches, parishioners bake special gluten-free bread out of concern for their brothers and sisters. Parishioners with CD often bring their own pieces of gluten-free wafers or crackers to be consecrated on the altar along with the usual bread. In other situations, congregations provide the gluten-free wafers and learn how to handle them with special care, as a pastoral ministry of the community.

If you are handling separate gluten-free bread, do not place it on the paten or in the ciborium with the regular bread. Keep the special pieces wrapped or in their own pyx near the set-apart chalice and far from the regular communion elements.

If the clergy and EMs have been handling the regular bread during the service, either for the consecration or distribution, their hands can cross-contaminate the special wafers. This is one reason to sanitize your hands after you have handled the bread when receiving communion yourself. Often it is best to offer the special wafer to the person from its own container without touching it yourself.

With a bit of ingenuity, clergy and EMs can help those who suffer find reverent and workable solutions. Talk with your parishioners struggling with celiac disease. Ask them to be specific about their needs when it comes to receiving the eucharist, and help them find a way to be included once again. Saying "All Are Welcome" in the Episcopal Church means going out of our way to minister to our brothers and sisters in Christ who kneel beside us at our altar rails every week.

CHAPTER 6

SPIRITUAL FORMATION

Eucharistic Ministers are congregational leaders and therefore role models for other Christians trying to live out their faith. This sacramental role is a large part of an EM's personal spirituality. This role also brings with it a responsibility to model spiritual leadership in your parish.

The blueprint for all Christian living is the Baptismal Covenant, which we reaffirm when others are baptized and on various holy days. All promise, with God's help:

- To continue in the apostles' teaching and fellowship, in the breaking of bread, and in the prayers;
- To persevere in resisting evil, and, whenever you fall into sin, repent and return to the Lord;
- To proclaim by word and example the Good News of God in Christ;
- To seek and serve Christ in all persons, loving your neighbor as yourself;
- To strive for justice and peace among all people, and respect the dignity of every human being. (BCP, p. 304–5)

■ HOLY HABITS

All of this certainly doesn't come naturally, so you must regularly exercise your many spiritual muscles to keep in shape. Theologian Caroline Westerhoff calls these "holy habits."

> As Christians we have heard and accepted the call into the grand and precarious quest of discipleship, and as disciples we are to become bold callers. The call has to do with habits—holy habits that direct us out of ourselves toward others and the Other. Habits that polish away the grit and grime we accumulate so readily. Habits that smooth the rough places that snag and tear. Habits that wash the imagination in fresh possibility. Habits that strengthen the spine and strengthen the heart. Habits that feed us and bring us cheer.[1]

Others refer to this idea as a "Rule of Life." Ask your clergy about the concept. They can point you to resources to help you develop a Rule that is right for you. A relationship with a spiritual director often can help bring order out of spiritual chaos and discipline where you need it, or even keep you on an even keel when you're spiritually out of sorts. If you are unfamiliar with the ministry of spiritual directors, ask your clergy or diocese to recommend those nearby. Some spiritual directors charge a small fee.

At the very minimum, Eucharistic Ministers should set an example by attending worship weekly, even (and especially) when not serving as an EM. Your presence through the church seasons and at special times, such as Holy Week, deepens your connection with the liturgy and thus your

---

1. Westerhoff, *Calling: A Song for the Baptized*, 5.

work as an EM. It is a spiritual discipline as well as a form of leadership.

Stay as involved with your congregation as you can, participating in parish events, outreach ministries, Sunday school, and other areas in which your gifts and talents are strongest.

EMs should plan daily prayer, perhaps giving time to Morning and Evening Prayer (now available electronically). My favorite website—dailyoffice.org—allows me to access these on my iPhone and iPad while I am on the go. (No app is available for this at the moment, and it is accessible to all computers!) All of the readings, extra prayers, and beautiful artwork make this BCP-less electronic experience holy. The site is also terrific for other Episcopal news, blogs, and information.

I also recommend a wise little book written especially for EMs, *Meditations for Lay Eucharistic Ministers* by Beth Maynard.[2]

Study is an important part of all Christians' spiritual disciplines. You should study the Scriptures in advance of the service to help you to enter into it with knowledge and anticipation. The sermon will make more sense to you, too! I love my library and the feel of my books in my hand. But my resources are limited by my book collection. I find the best way to study Scripture is online by using www. textweek.com. The website offers a gigantic compendium of commentaries; sermons; blogs; art; Greek and Hebrew word studies; writings from the Church Fathers and Mothers; and anything else you need to delve into God's Word. Everything is easy to find, conveniently catalogued, and

---

2. Beth Maynard, *Meditations for Lay Eucharistic Ministers* (Harrisburg, PA: Morehouse Publishing, 1999).

linked to specific readings in the church year. Poking around the site is a lot of fun. I learn something every time I visit the site!

Rest is also an important and oft-neglected part of your spiritual life. Burned-out EMs can't be fully present in their ministry at the altar rail. Learn to assess your own spiritual health. Take the biblical concept of Sabbath seriously. Days off are God's gift for recreation and "re-creation" that all humans need, especially those engaged in deep ministries. Longer periods of retreat nourish the body and the soul. Try a short, guided retreat if you never have experienced one. Clergy can recommend nearby places of refreshment that offer as much or as little expert spiritual guidance as you need.

If stressful things are happening in your work and/or family life, it is all right to take a break from eucharistic ministry or other activities. Talk with your clergy or spiritual director. Our lives have a rhythm, and so do all ministries. A hiatus can be healing. When both of my parents died unexpectedly within nine days of each other, I took six months off to get myself spiritually re-centered.

■ SURPRISE!

EMs often think of their ministry as one in which they give and others receive. Joy can take you by surprise in the routine sharing of the blood of Christ. You find yourself suddenly gazing into the sacred heart of things. A long-loved person touches the base of the chalice at the same time that you offer it, and your fingers brush. A stranger's clear blue eyes hold yours with such purity that you know you are gazing at Christ. Rainbows from stained glass fall across your hands cradling the cup. These moments are pure gift.

■ A WORD ABOUT ANXIETY

In the ministry of an EM, an infinite number of things can and do go "wrong." Most people who feel called to be an EM are the sort who strive to do everything "right," and that concern is made even greater by the holiness of the task at the altar rail. It is easy to fall prey to some amount of anxiety. Many laity called to this ministry decline to serve for fear of not knowing what to do or of making a mistake in front of the whole congregation. Preoccupation with "right and wrong" can interfere with your focus and your spirit as Christ's servant. The ministry can become all about performance instead of about the bread and wine—all about you instead of Christ's gift.

These are some of the many reasons EMs must keep themselves in spiritual shape. It is easy to give in to thoughts of "what will I do if . . . ?" No one can be prepared for everything. Our Lord and most of the people around you are concerned with your heart rather than your chalice technique.

■ SUPPORT AND CONTINUING EDUCATION

It helps to meet regularly with other EMs for support, problem-solving, information-sharing, and prayer. EMs from several congregations often gain a lot from sharing with each other. Only others who also enter into this complex sacramental ministry understand how it spiritually and emotionally impacts an EM.

Your continuing education is important for renewing your license[3] and, most importantly, for your continu-

---

3. *Constitution and Canons 2009*, III.4.2(b), 67. *http://www.episcopalarchives. org/pdf/CnC/CandC_2009pp65-121.pdf.*

ing spiritual growth. Your diocese probably offers several classes and levels of training for EMs.

Beyond that, pursue what interests you. This is what Westerhoff refers to at the beginning of this chapter as "habits that feed us and bring us cheer."[4] Pay attention to the Holy Spirit's nudging to further explore Scripture, or sacramental theology, or English church history, or medieval stained glass, or gardening, or any of thousands of wonders that attract you and deepen your spiritual life.

Perhaps this book piqued your curiosity about a topic. No doubt your own Bible study will guide you onto unexpected paths. Your spirit will never cease to hunger for God.

I close this chapter on spiritual formation with a Roman Catholic priest's prayerful musings on the chalice, perfect for a Eucharistic Minister's meditation:

> Like a chalice consecrated for use at Mass, the Incarnation, followed by our incorporation into the Body of Christ by Baptism, sets us apart as a holy people. We no longer belong to a profane world, but to God. In the world but not of the world (John 17:16), we have been consecrated and belong to the Father through Christ. And like the sacred vessels at Mass, we are destined by divine decree to receive the body, blood, soul and divinity of Jesus Christ.[5]

---

4. Westerhoff, *Calling: A Song for the Baptized*, 5.

5. Jerry Pokorsky, "The Veil, the Chalice and the Dignity of Man: Like the Sacred Vessels at Mass, We Were Made to Receive Christ," *Adoremus Bulletin* 2, no. 9 (February 1997): accessed January 22, 2012, *http://www.adoremus. org/0297VeilChalice.html*.

CHAPTER 7

SOME QUESTIONS AND A FEW ANSWERS

M any congregations task Eucharistic Ministers with a variety of other ministries—mainly lector, acolyte, and Eucharistic Visitor. In other parishes, particularly those without a deacon, an EM might be appointed to assume many of the traditional tasks of that order—setting up and cleaning up the altar, leading prayers of the people, carrying the gospel book in the procession, holding it for the gospel reader. Here is a partial list of things an EM needs to consider (for the ministry of EM only) before each service.

■ BEFORE A SERVICE . . .

❑ What vestments do I need to wear?

❑ Have I turned my cell phone off and left it in a secure place?

❑ Have I used the toilet and washed my hands?

❑ Is there anything about this particular service that is unusual?

❑ Have I looked over the service bulletin to be sure there will be no surprises?

- ❑ Which eucharistic service are we doing?
- ❑ Where are my Book of Common Prayer, necessary hymnal(s), and service bulletin?
- ❑ Should I carry them in procession or put them in my seat ahead of time?
- ❑ Where is my place in the procession?
- ❑ Where do I sit during the service?
- ❑ Where am I to be during the liturgy of the table?
- ❑ When do I stand and/or kneel?
- ❑ When and where should I take my own communion after the consecration?
- ❑ Where is the hand sanitizer in the chancel?
- ❑ Which chalice will I be using and am I familiar with it?
- ❑ With whom am I paired for communion?
- ❑ Which parts of the altar rail will I be responsible for?
- ❑ How will I get more wine?
- ❑ Will I fill my own chalice?
- ❑ Where are the extra purificators?
- ❑ Will I help commune people in the pews who cannot come forward?
- ❑ What should I do with my leftover wine and used purificator?
- ❑ Where should I stand or sit when I am finished at the rail?
- ❑ Do I leave in the procession?

WHAT TO WEAR?

Participants wear vestments at most church services so that their clothing does not detract attention from the most important activity—the worship of God.

Most parishes have their own customs about what EMs wear, usually a cassock and surplice, or an alb and cincture. If at all possible, EMs should be a vested part of the altar party because they are serving an integral liturgical function.

Appearance is important whatever you wear. Make sure that the robe you choose grazes the tops of your shoes. A robe that is too long is dangerous; a robe that falls somewhere between your knees and ankles can't help but draw stares.

Some parishes have special crosses for EMs to wear over their vestments. Some EMs like to wear their own crosses, but ask your clergy first to see if that's OK. Keep in mind that the goal is to blend in, so try not to wear anything that markedly differentiates you when you are vested. If your necklace is ornamental (pearls, for instance), tuck it under your vestments. In general, do not pin or clip something to the outside of what you are wearing. Name tags; vestry or Daughters of the King pins; colored ribbons of support groups; and buttons advertizing the parish retreat all detract from the service; they call attention to you and noticeably differentiate you from other participants.

In that spirit, also take an inventory of your jewelry and your hands, both of which are at eye level to most communicants when you offer the cup. Strange-colored, glittery, or chipped nail polish might detract from your ministry. Clanking bracelets, large or numerous rings, dangling earrings, and the like also draw unwanted attention.

EMs' shoes are highly visible beneath vestments! (Who hasn't seen a young acolyte wearing flip flops?!) Fairly dressy, dark shoes (with minimal bling!) and plain dark socks are best. Women traditionally do not wear open-toed shoes in the chancel.

The right shoes also are important for comfort and safety. If you have to negotiate several levels in your chancel, high heels are risky. Wear your most comfortable shoes, especially if it's a longer service such as Christmas and Easter.

In congregations where nonvested EMs come from out of the congregation, the same principles of dress apply to keeping the focus on the eucharist rather than your attire.

In more relaxed settings—worship that is outdoors or at a camp or conference center—dress for EMs (and most service participants) would be more relaxed, and even EMs might be able to get away with flip flops!

■ WHAT DO I DO IF SOMEONE AT THE ALTAR RAIL . . .

1. Has her arms crossed in an X over her chest . . .

This usually means that the person may have taken the bread but does not want to receive the wine. If you know that the communicant has taken the bread but does not take the wine, then say the sentence of administration but do not offer the cup. Or she may be waiting for a blessing (ordinarily if a priest or a bishop is distributing the bread, he would have blessed her), in which case you can stop in front of her and say something like, "May the Lord bless us and keep us." A third-person phrase is appropriate, but please do not trace the cross on the communicant's forehead or lay your hand on her head; these are liturgical signs reserved for priests and bishops.

2. Opens her mouth wide and sticks her tongue out . . .

This usually means that she wants to commune by intinction. Take her wafer, dip it lightly in the chalice, and place it on her tongue, being careful to keep your fingers out of the wine and not to touch her mouth or tongue.

TAKING YOUR EUCHARIST

"The ministers receive the Sacrament in both kinds, and then immediately deliver it to the people" (BCP, p. 365). Just as the clergy in the altar party take communion from the bread and wine consecrated during the service before offering it to others, so Eucharistic Ministers should take communion before performing their ministry. Make a point of learning from your clergy before the service begins exactly when you should come forward and where you will receive.

3. Is holding a wafer . . .

This normally means that the person wants to receive by intinction. Ideally, you as the EM should be the one to dip the bread into the cup and place it on the person's tongue. If the communicant makes a move toward the cup with the wafer, lower the cup to a level where she can see inside it to lightly dip. If the communicant seems confused about what to do with the bread, either indicate to her that she should consume it or gently take it for intinction.

4. Won't let go of his bread . . .

This may mean he wants to dip the wafer himself. Do not try to take it from him at the altar rail, even if you have been taught that EMs are the ones who dip the bread and place it in communicants' mouths. Lower the chalice and allow him to dip and consume his own bread. If the parish or diocesan policy precludes self-intinction, let the rector know after the service so she can address this appropriately with the parishioner. The time to explain policy is generally not during communion.

5. Shakes her head "no" . . .

The communicant is most likely signaling that she already has had the wine or that she does not receive the wine. If her arms are crossed over her chest, *see no. 1 above*.

6. Tries to take the chalice from me . . .

As you have more and more experience as an EM, you will learn which techniques work for you for administering the cup. A firm grip is essential, but too firm a grip can be awkward and makes it too hard for the communicant to get any wine. The caveat is to keep a firm grip on the cup but don't wrestle a communicant for it! If the person is determined to hold it himself, relinquish it but keep a careful eye on it so that you or the communicant do not drop it or spill wine transferring it back and forth.

> *Tip:* Clergy attending the service who are not vested and who commune at the rail often expect by virtue of their office to take the chalice from you and commune themselves.

7. Doesn't help guide the chalice . . .

Many new Episcopalians mistakenly believe that they should not touch the chalice. As an EM, you know that this hands-off approach makes your ministry harder. It is OK to quietly indicate that he should lightly grasp the base of the chalice to help guide it.

8. Grasps the stem or the bowl of the cup rather than the edge . . .

Situations like this underscore your need to stay focused and retain control of the chalice so that the wine does not slosh out of the chalice. Unfortunately, there is little warning that this situation is about to occur.

9. Spills wine on herself or himself . . .

Hand the purificator to the person to dab at the wine on him or herself. I once observed my sweet elderly father in the role of EM dabbing at a matriarch's considerable bosom with a purificator. If the spill is a large one, you might have to indicate to the communicant that she can hold on to the linen until after the service. Get a clean purificator so that you can continue. Remember to retrieve the soaked purificator after the service because the consecrated wine on it needs to be properly cleaned.

10. Spills wine on the altar rail . . .

If wine spills on the altar rail, immediately wipe it up with the purificator. After the service, go back and clean the area with a purificator and water. Tell a member of the altar guild about the spill so she can properly clean the purificator(s) you have used and double-check the spill area.

11. Spills wine on the floor or kneeler or carpet . . .

If the consecrated wine ends up on a small area of the floor in front of the person receiving, immediately blot up what you can with the purificator, fetch a clean linen, and continue to serve. Return after the service to clean up more thoroughly with water. If the spill is large, you might have to close down a portion of the altar rail until it has been cleaned.

If the wine spills on the carpet or kneeler, blot up what you can and place the purificator over the blotted spill. Obtain a clean purificator and continue to serve, more thoroughly cleaning up after the service as above. Again, remember to tell an altar guild member about the spill so that she can properly clean the purificator(s) you have used and double-check the spill area.

12. Drops her bread on the floor . . .

Pick it up immediately. An EM may consume it himself, give it to a priest to consume, or keep it in his purificator. Indicate to the paten bearer that the congregant needs another wafer and then offer the cup. Set the purificator containing the bread on the credence table for the altar guild to deal with after the liturgy. Also tell the person performing the closing ablutions about the host folded up in the linen.

13. Is chewing gum or a mint . . .

Ask him to remove it from his mouth before drinking from the chalice.

14. Drops chewing gum into the chalice . . .

I know EMs who have faced this dilemma! That chalice should no longer be used until it is sterilized. Tell a priest or deacon what has happened and hand the tainted chalice over or place it where directed on the altar or credence table, draping your purificator over it to signal that it is consecrated but out of use.

15. Drops her wafer into the chalice . . .

This can happen when a communicant is attempting self-intinction. There are several ways to handle it:

1. If you ever wondered why sometimes there is a spoon on the altar, now you know one of the reasons! Use it to fish the wafer out of the cup and put the soggy bread into your purificator. Help the person obtain another piece of bread and re-offer the cup. Get a clean purificator as soon as possible.

2. If you are near the paten bearer, ask for a wafer and use that dry wafer to fish out the host in the cup. Put both wafers onto the communicant's tongue. (This technique is most effective when the chalice is less full!)

3. Use a dry corner of your purificator to try to fish it out and bundle the bread into the purificator. Obtain another consecrated wafer from the paten and offer the cup. As soon as possible, put the soggy linen on the credence table and get a clean one.

Under no circumstances should the EM or the communicant try to pick the bread from the chalice with his fingers.

Often it is difficult to remove the bread from a tulip-shaped chalice. If you cannot get the bread out after a reasonable attempt, the EM must retire the chalice from service, placing it on the altar or credence table with your purificator draped over it. Be aware that you probably are holding up the process at the rail as you are doing this.

16. Shares her bread with someone else . . .

We occasionally see this practice between parent and child. You might have to ask the adult if the child receives the wine also. This sharing is a nice gesture, though theologically each should have her own wafer. The rector or vicar could address this privately with the family at another time.

17. Tries to take the bread when he leaves the rail . . .

I have seen this happen with children and occasionally with adults. If it's possible to do so subtly, indicate that she should eat the wafer or give it back to you. Tell the presider after the service so that she can follow up appropriately.

18. Hands the bread back to me . . .

Obviously this is not the time to ask why. Accept the bread and, remembering that it is consecrated, place it on the altar or credence table. Let the presider or deacon know why it is there. Some EMs are taught to wrap the bread in their purificator and continue until they have gotten to a stopping place and can get a clean purificator.

19. Indicates that he hasn't yet received the host . . .

Get a paten bearer's attention so that he can serve the person or indicate to the communicant to wait for the paten bearer's next "pass."

20. Hits her teeth on the chalice . . .

This usually causes a loud clang. It hurts and can even draw blood. If that is the case, hand the purificator to the person to take with her. Discern if the person is all right, and if not, beckon to a nearby usher to take care of the situation. Be sure to retrieve the used purificator.

21. Wants another sip . . .

Offer the cup again because sometimes a communicant can't get a sip of the wine because of the angle of the chalice (especially if the level of the wine is low).

22. Begins talking with me . . .

Since communion is not an appropriate time or place for such communication, simply smile and quietly say "later" or "not now." Many communicants have tried to convey a message to me such as "I'm feeling better!" or "Mrs. So-and-so is in the hospital and wants you to bring her communion after church" or "I need to talk with you after the service." My young son once asked me at the altar rail, "What are we having for lunch?"

23. Grabs my hand . . .

Gently disengage your hand and assure the communicant you will talk with her after the service.

24. Faints or gets sick . . .

Get the attention of an usher, who will help the person. That's one of the ministries of an usher!

25. Has piercings on her mouth or tongue . . .

That person probably knows how to negotiate drinking from a cup, so it should not be a problem for an EM. It might be better if that person used intinction instead for sanitary reasons. But do not suggest this at the altar rail. Make the rector aware of your concerns after the service.

26. Wants me to give her a blessing . . .

The altar rail is no place for a long explanation of why a layperson cannot do this. A third-person phrase asking for God's blessing—"May the Lord bless us and keep us"—would offer comfort to that person. *See no. 1 above.*

27. Responds with something other than "Amen" . . .

Though "Amen" is the accepted response *before* taking each element, many people are not aware of that. Often parishioners will respond after drinking from the cup. Besides "Amen," you likely will hear "Thanks!" or "Thank you!" I also have heard "Awesome!" and "God bless you." They may not be aware of it, but communicants are acknowledging in their own ways a genuine appreciation of God's gift of the blood of Christ that you offer to them. This is not really a response to you as a person, so there's no need to say "You're welcome," which I have heard from some EMs at the rail. A smile and a nod of agreement will show them that you have heard their exclamation of thanksgiving.

▇ WHAT DO I DO IF I . . .

28. Drop someone's bread into the cup while giving intinction . . .
See No. 15 above.

29. Spill consecrated wine on the floor or altar rail . . .
See no. 10 above.

30. Spill consecrated wine on the kneeler or the carpet . . .
See no. 11 above.

31. Spill consecrated wine on someone . . .
See no. 9 above.

32. Drop someone's bread on the floor . . .
See no. 12 above.

33. Drop the chalice . . .
This is the ultimate horror for any EM. It is comforting to know that this mishap is rare. I have never seen an EM do this, but I have seen it happen to a priest. A chalice generally makes a very loud noise when it hits the floor, particularly if the cup is silver and the floor is uncarpeted. The chalice can be dented or broken. A pottery cup is particularly likely to shatter if it is dropped on a floor instead of carpet. In any case, an EM's task is to soak up the spilled wine as

quickly as possible, particularly if the wine is consecrated. You may need several purificators to accomplish this. The chalice should be retired for the rest of the service for sanitary reasons.

34. Find that my purificator is dirty or soaked with wine . . .

Get a clean one as soon as you can.

35. Abstain from alcoholic beverages myself . . .

Before the service, let the presider and your fellow EMs know that you do not receive the cup yourself and will not be able to drain the chalice you are using, if that is an expectation of the parish or diocese.

36. Need to say something to a communicant . . .

As a general rule, any conversation between you and a communicant should be as quick and quiet as possible. Gestures are preferable to words. A person's reception of the body and blood is the most sacred moment of the service. As an EM you should keep in mind while doing your duties that you will be surrounded by people who are in the midst of this holy experience and keep from disturbing them as best you can.

37. Need to leave the service suddenly . . .
Or
Get sick, feel faint, or faint . . .

If you can, put your chalice down on the altar or hand it to someone in the altar party and leave by the nearest exit. Be sure to tell someone that you are feeling unwell and are leaving. If you feel faint or too hot, it's best to sit down or leave instead of pushing on and risking a fainting spell while holding a full chalice.

38. Run out of wine and need more . . .

Each congregation handles this in its own way. An EM needs to be familiar with her parish's routine and to be clear on this before the service.

Here are some of the options you could have: 1) A deacon is often assigned to refill chalices; 2) or an acolyte does this duty; 3) or an assisting priest can do this; 4) or a verger often takes this role; or 5) the EM approaches the altar to do it herself.

If you are refilling your chalice yourself:

Make sure you know which is the consecrated wine; sometimes a container of unconsecrated wine is left on the altar or credence table. If you are not sure, ask someone.

It's a ripe time for spills. It helps to hold your purificator under the spout of the cruet or decanter to catch any drops as you pour into your chalice.

Take only the amount of wine that you estimate you will need for the remainder of communion. Be sure you have some extra in your cup. If they are presented with a nearly empty chalice, the last few communicants tend to only let the wine touch their lips, which is unsanitary.

If you use the last of the consecrated wine, be sure to let the celebrant and the other EMs know.

If someone else is refilling your chalice for you:

It is helpful if that person monitors the amount in EMs' chalices so that he can be ready to refill yours. You may have to get his attention, though.

If you can, place the cup on the altar or credence table for stability while it is being refilled. If your chalice is refilled while you are holding it at the rail, pay attention to the amount. Tell the person how much you need. Be ready with your own purificator to catch any drips.

Refills are handled differently if you are at a communion station in another area of the building.

39. Find that my chalice is too full . . .

Turning your back to the congregation, drink the wine down to a suitable level so that you will not spill it as you walk.

40. Have too much wine left over to drink by myself . . .

Know your parish's policy on this. Now that we as a society are so mindful of alcohol abuse, many congregations are choosing not to have EMs drain their chalices but to put the vessel on the credence table and cover it with a purificator for proper disposal later. In other places, if the custom is for the EM to finish the cup, if it's too much, ask a fellow EM or one of the clergy to help you. Under NO circumstances should you ask an acolyte to assist you with finishing the cup unless that person is an adult.

41. See that I am going to run out of wine and there is no more consecrated wine available . . .

If you are administering the only cup at the service, ask the presider or deacon if additional consecrated wine is in the aumbry or tabernacle. If there is not, the presider may decide to consecrate more. If you are serving with other EMs and you are toward the end of the service, one of them may have enough wine to finish communing those at your portion of the rail. When you get near the last of the wine in your chalice and you know there is no more, do not allow it to get empty for sanitary reasons. Your fellow EM(s) will finish for you.

42. Get way behind the person giving the bread and am holding up the people at the altar rail . . .

Or

Keep having to wait for the paten bearer to catch up with me . . .

This is a very important and often overlooked problem. Both of these situations are a matter of pace and often are hard to navigate with reverence and dignity. An EM should try to match the pace of the paten bearer whom he is following. This might not always be a comfortable pace for you, but you neither want to crowd that person by going faster than he is, nor hold things up by being slow in your task. If at all possible, leave two communicants between you and the person with the paten. In practical terms: If there are four people in a row at the altar rail, the EM should not start to offer the cup to no. 1 until the person with the paten has communed nos. 1, 2, and 3. When she begins to give bread to no. 4, the EM should offer the wine to no. 1. This also keeps both ministers of communion from crowding each other where the altar rail meets a wall.

43. Don't know where my side of the altar rail ends and another EM's side begins . . .

Or

Don't know where at the altar rail to start and stop giving the cup . . .

This should be clear before the service begins. If you are confused when you get into the chancel, quietly signal to or ask another EM.

44. Realize that I am using a corporal or lavabo towel instead of a purificator . . .

This happens way too often. Congratulations! You can tell the difference between them! A purificator is an EM's primary tool; its shape and folds are ideally suited to wiping the chalice. At your first opportunity, return to where the extra purificators are kept and choose the proper linen. Leave your old linen crumpled on the credence table and let the deacon or presider and altar guild know why it is there.

45. Hear my cell phone ring or need to check it during the service . . .

If it rings, shut it off immediately.

Do not, under ANY circumstances, look at or use your cell phone when you are serving as an EM! If you are awaiting an emergency call or text, you should not be serving at the altar. Your attention and focus will be elsewhere. If you are a person who habitually checks your phone, do not even take it into the service with you.

As a general rule, since your cell phone should be off—not merely on vibrate—there is no need to take it into the service with you.

BIBLIOGRAPHY

Aquilina, Mike. *The Mass of the Early Christians.* Huntington, IN: Our Sunday Visitor, 2001.

Aquinas, Thomas. *Summa Theologica.* Translated by Fathers of the English Dominican Province. Vol. III.82.13. New York: Benziger Brothers, 1947.

"The Ardagh Chalice," The National Museum of Ireland. *http://www. museum.ie/en/list/artefacts.aspx?article=bfcd87b3-c3b1-489c-84- f3-5c8bc08cc471,* accessed December 28, 2011.

Augustin of Hippo. "Letter 138" 1.7. Translated by Marcus Dods. In *Nicene and Post-Nicene Fathers of the Christian Church.* Series I, volume I. Edited by Philip Schaff. Edinburgh: T&T Clark, 1886. *http://www.ccel.org/ccel/schaff/npnf101.pdf,* accessed January 29, 2012.

————. "Lectures or Tractates on the Gospel of John" 5:18. Translated by John Gibb and James Innes. In *Nicene and Post-Nicene Fathers of the Christian Church.* Series I, vol. VII. Edited by Philip Schaff. Edinburgh: T&T Clark, 1888. *http://www.ccel.org/ccel/ schaff/npnf107.pdf,* accessed January 29, 2012.

Basil the Great. "Letter 93." Translated by Blomfield Jackson. In *Nicene and Post-Nicene Fathers of the Christian Church.* Series II, vol. III. Edited by Philip Schaff and Henry Wace. Edinburgh: T&T Clark, 1894. *http://www.ccel.org/ccel/schaff/npnf208.pdf,* accessed January 2, 2012.

Buechner, Frederick. *Wishful Thinking: A Theological ABC.* New York: Harper & Row, 1973.

Christian Formation Committee of the Diocesan Commission on Ministry. *Liturgical Ministries Profiles: A Customary for The Episcopal Diocese of Vermont.* Episcopal Diocese of Vermont, 2006. *http://www.dioceseofvermont.org/Resources/COM/Liturgi- calMinProfiles.pdf,* accessed December 5, 2011.

Communion in the Hand is a Sacrilege. These Last Days Ministries, 2012. *http://www.tldm.org/news2/cih.htm,* accessed April 2, 2012.

Cyril of Jerusalem. "Mystagogical Catechesis" V:21-22. Translated by Edwin Hamilton Gifford. In *Nicene and Post-Nicene Fathers of the Christian Church*. Series II, vol. VII. Edited by Philip Schaff and Henry Wace. Edinburgh: T&T Clark, 1893. *http://www.ccel. org/ccel/schaff/npnf207.pdf*, accessed January 4, 2012.

Donkin, T. C. *An Etymological Dictionary of the Romance Languages: Chiefly from the German of Friedrich Dietz*. London: Williams & Norgate, 1864.

Donne, John. "On the Sacrament." In *Remembering the Faith: What Christians Believe*, by Douglas J. Brouwer. Grand Rapids, MI: Wm. B. Eerdmans Publishing, 1999.

Ely, Beth Wickenberg. *A Manual for Eucharistic Visitors*. Harrisburg, PA: Morehouse Publishing, 2005.

The Episcopal Church. *The Book of Common Prayer and Administration of the Sacraments and Other Rites and Ceremonies of the Church*. New York: Church Hymnal Corp., 1979.

———. *The Book of Common Prayer and the Administration of the Sacraments and Other Rites and Ceremonies of the Church According to the Use of The Protestant Episcopal Church in the United States of America*. New York: The Church Pension Fund, 1928.

———. *The Book of Occasional Services 2003*. New York: Church Publishing, 2003.

———. *Constitution and Canons . . . for The Episcopal Church 2009*. New York: Church Publishing Inc., 2010. *http://www.episcopalarchives.org/CnC_ToC_2009.html*.

———. *The Hymnal*. New York: Church Hymnal Corp., 1982.

Episcopal Diocese of Arkansas. *Guidelines on Ministration to the Sick in the Episcopal Church in Arkansas*. Episcopal Diocese of Arkansas. Revised April 29, 2008. *http://Episcopalarkansas.org/wp-content/uploads/2010/06/Ministry-to-the-sick-guidelines.pdf*, accessed January 2, 2012.

Episcopal Diocese of Oregon. "Discernment Brochure 2010." Episcopal Diocese of Oregon website, 2010. *http://www.episcopaldioceseoregon.org/files/discernment_brochure_2010.pdf,* accessed January 22, 2012.

General Instruction of the Roman Missal (Third Typical Edition). Translated by the International Committee on English in the Liturgy. Washington, DC: United States Catholic Conference, 2003.

House of Bishops of the Church of England. *The Eucharist: Sacrament of Unity*. London: Church Publishing Company, 2001.

Jefferts Schori, Katharine. *A Wing and a Prayer: A Message of Faith and Hope.* Harrisburg, PA: Morehouse, 2007.

Journal of the General Convention of the Episcopal Church, Minneapolis, 1976. New York: General Convention, 1977.

Journal of the General Convention of the Episcopal Church, Anaheim, 1985. New York: General Convention, 1986.

Journal of the General Convention of The Episcopal Church, Detroit, 1988. New York: General Convention, 1989.

Journal of the General Convention of The Episcopal Church, Philadelphia, 1997. New York: General Convention, 1998.

Journal of the General Convention of The Episcopal Church, Minneapolis, 2003. New York: General Convention, 2004.

Journal of the General Convention of the Episcopal Church, Anaheim, 2009. New York : General Convention, 2010.

LeClercq, Henri and Fernand Cabrol. "Communion." In *Dictionnaire d'Archéologie Chrétienne et de Liturgie.* Vol. 3, part 2. Paris: Librarie Letouzey et Ané, 1948.

Legg, J. Wickham, ed. *English Orders for Consecrating Churches in the Seventeenth Century.* London: Harrison & Sons, 1911.

Loving, Anne LaGrange, et al. "The Effects of Receiving Holy Communion on Health." *Journal of Environmental Health* 60, no. 1 (July/August 1997): 6–10.

Manangan, Lilia P., Lynne M. Sehulster, Linda Chiarello, Dawn N. Simonds, et al. "Risk of Infectious Disease Transmission from a Common Communion Cup." *American Journal of Infection Control* 26, no. 5 (October 1998): 538–39.

Martons, Joseph. "What Are Sacraments?" *Catholic Update,* n.d. *http://www.americancatholic.org/newsletters/cu/ac0895.asp.*

Maynard, Beth. *Meditations for Lay Eucharistic Ministers.* Harrisburg, PA: Morehouse Publishing, 1999.

Pokorsky, Jerry. "The Veil, the Chalice and the Dignity of Man: Like the Sacred Vessels at Mass, We Were Made to Receive Christ." *Adoremus Bulletin* 2, no. 9 (February 1997). *http://www.adoremus.org/0297VeilChalice.html,* accessed January 22, 2012.

Sisk, Mark S. and Catherine S. Roskam. *Healthcare Concerns and Liturgical Practices: A Memorandum to the Priests and Deacons of the Diocese.* Episcopal Diocese of New York. September 2009. *http://www.dioceseny.org/pages/443-healthcare-concerns-and-liturgical-practices,* accessed October 14, 2011.

Standing Commission on Ministry Development. "Toward a Theology of Ministry." Task Group on the Theology of Baptismal and Ordained Ministry, Archives of The Episcopal Church, 2000. *http://archive.episcopalchurch.org/documents/Toward_a_Theology_of_Ministry.pdf.*

Taylor, Jeremy. "Of the Real Presence of Christ in the Holy Sacrament." In *The Whole Works of the Right Reverend Jeremy Taylor.* Vol. VI, sec. I. Edited by Reginald Heber. Revised by Charles Page Eden. London: Longman, Brown, Green, and Longmans, 1852.

Thurston, Herbert. "Chalice." In *The Catholic Encyclopedia.* Vol. III. Edited by Kevin Knight. New York: Robert Appleton Co., 1908. *http://www.newadvent.org/cathen/03561a.htm,* accessed October 23, 2011.

Warner, Gerald, and Stephen Klimczuk. *Secret Places, Hidden Sanctuaries: Uncovering Mysterious Sights, Symbols, and Societies.* New York: Sterling Publishing, 2009.

Westerhoff, Caroline A. *Calling: A Song for the Baptized.* Harrisburg, PA: Seabury Classics, 2005.

www.ingramcontent.com/pod-product-compliance
Lightning Source LLC
Jackson TN
JSHW081318130125
77033JS00011B/342